HIDDEN HISTORY

HISTORY

of the

LAUREL

HIGHLANDS

D1519210

HIDDEN HISTORY

of the

LAUREL HIGHLANDS

Cassandra Vivian

THE
History
PRESS

Published by The History Press
Charleston, SC 29403
www.historypress.net

Front cover: Northern Italian men at the NIPA hall in Monessen. *Courtesy of the author.*
Back cover, top: Miners at a pit entrance. *Courtesy of Bill Hare.*
Back cover, bottom: Tollhouse at Addison. *Courtesy of the author.*

First published 2014

Manufactured in the United States

ISBN 978.1.62619.677.3

Library of Congress CIP data applied for.

To the people of the Laurel Highlands: the Native Americans, the pioneers, the immigrants, the farmers, the coal miners, the steel workers, the river men and their storytellers. They were our ancestors. They built America. We do not honor them enough.

Contents

CONTENTS

Preface

Every author wonders what will happen to the dozens if not hundreds of short articles, magazine and newspaper commissions and other pieces of their work. They were published once. Now they languish, perhaps never to be read again. Some of them are among the best of their writing, but who will find them, enjoy them and share them after the author passes away? I have hundreds of such works. Their topics cover three distinct genres: Egypt, Italian-Americana and local history.

I lived in and wrote about Egypt for nearly half of my life, and much of that writing, I fear, will never see the light of day again. The two books I wrote, *The Western Desert of Egypt: An Explorer's Handbook* and *Americans in Egypt, 1770–1915* have found their place in the literature of Egypt; but the dozens of articles may just fade away forever, especially in these turbulent times in the Middle East.

I researched and recorded my family's immigrant experience and wrote about food, customs and traditions in short articles and several books including *A Tuscan-American Kitchen* and *The Overseer's Family*. My research extended to my hometown and region, and that gave birth to a host of articles that, once published, were searching for a home.

But here, in this cleverly imagined book, at least part of the work that I did about my hometown and region will have a home.

I love to write. I taught research and writing at the university level on two continents. Research is like a giant treasure hunt. There is always an amazing story to discover. This book is filled with such stories. Many more are tucked back in history waiting to be discovered. *The Hungarian Women of Morewood* is an amazing story. So is *A Mount Pleasant Hero*. Sometimes my research does not find the answer. That is true for *A Frick Observatory and a Brashear Telescope*. Its mystery continues. In fact, most of the stories in this book are fascinating glimpses in history. History is mesmerizing.

Acknowledgements

How does one acknowledge all the help received for numerous articles written over a number of decades? It is impossible. So, thank you to all of you who answered questions, resolved mysteries and generally encouraged me to write these articles. You know who you are and I know who you are, and although your name is not printed here, it is remembered.

Most of the very short stories in this book were first published in the local newspaper in a column called "Our Town Remembered" that was designed for the Mount Pleasant Area Historical Society. Two articles on coal and a third on Braddock Road first appeared in *Crossroads Magazine*, an organ of the Fayette County Cultural Trust. The article on Italians in Monessen first appeared in *Il Primo* magazine. The article on Frick at the World's Fair was written for the Westmoreland County Historical Society's magazine called *Westmoreland History*. There are a few original articles, especially on Somerset County. The map of the Laurel Highlands is courtesy of the Laurel Highlands Visitor's Bureau.

Introduction

The Laurel Highlands is not all ski resorts and famous trolley parks. It is so much more than that. It is centuries of history. It is explorers and pioneers looking for the American dream. It is Native Americans trying to hold on to theirs. It is the story of European immigrants and their role in creating the Industrial Revolution that built America. Their story is of coal and how it was mined and who mined it; of steel as it was used to build a nation; of glass and its reflective beauty; of the paths, trails and roads that crisscrossed the region; and of the streams and rivers that flowed north instead of south and made the region the fulcrum of the nation.

Yes, the people are the story of the Laurel Highlands. The colorful and fascinating people who still cling to their ethnic churches in defiance of the religious leaders, still have ethnic clubs where members congregate regularly to celebrate who they are and still participate in community festivals where thousands of people gather to eat their special foods and dance their traditional dances. That is the Laurel Highlands you will find in this book.

The Laurel Highlands consists of three counties in southwestern Pennsylvania: Fayette, Somerset and Westmoreland. This book is divided on similar lines. The first section of the book is called "Around the Highlands" and tells the stories that belong to the entire highland: migration, immigration, coal, steel, glass and families. The remainder of the book is divided by county. Fayette County is ancient roads, boatbuilding, more coal mines and intriguing towns with extraordinary buildings. Somerset County is maple trees and, unfortunately, earth-shattering disasters. Westmoreland

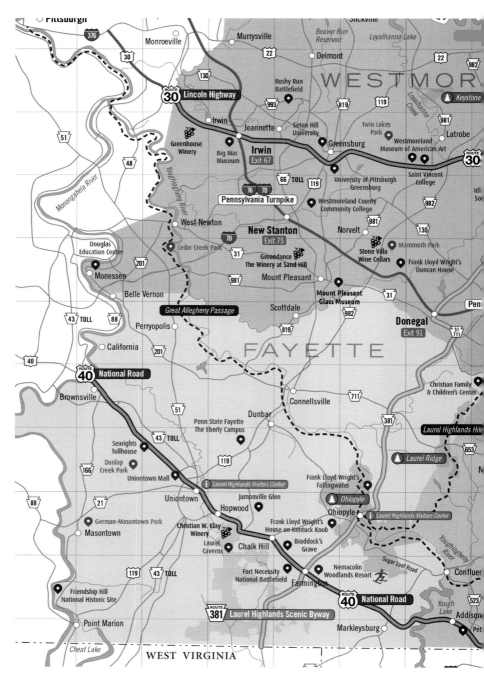

A map of the Laurel Highlands. *Courtesy of the Laurel Highlands Visitors Bureau.*

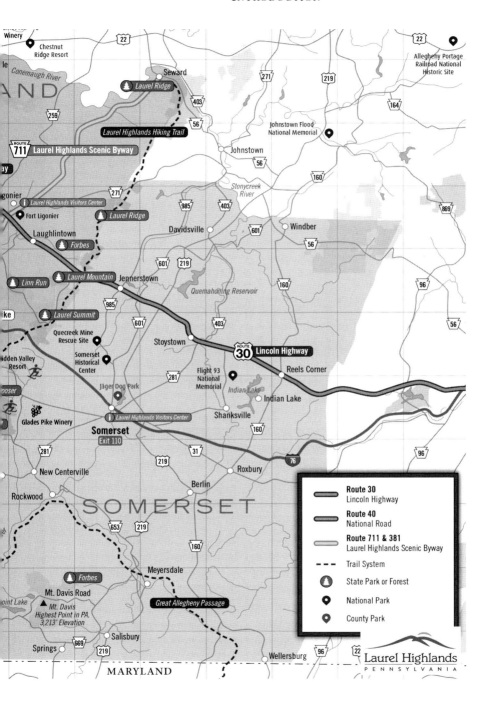

Winery
Chestnut
Ridge Resort
Conemaugh River
AND
Seward
Laurel Ridge
Laurel Highlands Hiking Trail
ROUTE 711 Laurel Highlands Scenic Byway
gonier
Laurel Highlands Visitors Center
Fort Ligonier
Laughlintown
Forbes
Linn Run
Laurel Mountain
Jennerstown
Laurel Summit
ike
Quecreek Mine
Rescue Site
Somerset
Historical
Center
idden Valley
Resort
ooser
Jäger Dog Park
Glades Pike Winery
Laurel Highlands Visitors Center
Somerset
Exit 110
New Centerville
Rockwood
SOMERSET
Mt. Davis Road
Forbes
Mt. Davis
int Lake
Highest Point in PA.
3,213' Elevation
Salisbury
Springs
MARYLAND

Chestnut
Seward
Johnstown Flood
National Memorial
Johnstown
Stonycreek
River
Davidsville
Windber
Quemahoning Reservoir
Stoystown
Lincoln Highway
Reels Corner
Flight 93
National
Memorial
Indian Lake
Indian Lake
Shanksville
Roxbury
Berlin
Meyersdale
Great Allegheny Passage
Wellersburg

Allegheny Portage
Railroad National
Historic Site

Route numbers: 22, 271, 219, 164, 403, 259, 56, 711, 271, 985, 403, 869, 601, 56, 601, 219, 160, 96, 985, 56, 601, 403, 30, 281, 31, 219, 76, 96, 281, 653, 219, 160, 669, 219, 96, 22

Legend:
Route 30
Lincoln Highway
Route 40
National Road
Route 711 & 381
Laurel Highlands Scenic Byway
- - - Trail System
State Park or Forest
National Park
County Park

Laurel Highlands
PENNSYLVANIA

County is more ancient roads leading to an incredible river whose commerce fed lumber, steel and more to the nation.

You are about to begin an interesting journey—sometimes sad, sometimes funny, always captivating. I hope you enjoy reading about it as much as I enjoyed researching and writing it.

I

Around the Highlands

THE MYSTERIOUS BRADDOCK ROAD IN PENNSYLVANIA

We may never know the exact route of the road that General Braddock and his men built along the Monongahela River in 1755 on their way to defeat, especially its southwestern Pennsylvania portion. After all, it has been nearly three hundred years since the British Army carved its path through the swamps and primeval forests of Fayette and Westmoreland Counties on its way to take Fort DuQuesne away from the French. It was an important mission, for whoever controlled the confluence of the Monongahela and Allegheny Rivers as they formed the Ohio controlled the gateway to most of the continent.

Modern researchers read the various accounts written by the men of the army. They pore over the letters of George Washington and the journals of Christopher Gist, both of whom blazed the trail earlier and accompanied Braddock as he made his ill-fated journey. The problem is that most of the literature does not give much detail about the Pennsylvania portion of the journey, especially from the crossing of the Youghiogheny River at Connellsville to the route through Mount Pleasant Borough and East Huntingdon Township. In addition, the little that we do have has created some disagreement among the scholars.

Braddock's Army marching to Fort DuQuesne. *Courtesy of the author.*

The final components in the quest for Braddock Road are the people who live along its course, especially those whose families have researched the route through generations. They have their own beliefs as to the direction it took, sometimes contradicting what the scholars have to say. The local people know the secrets of the road: the location of springs, the changes in the terrain and the changes that have taken place through the years. They back up their beliefs not only with artifacts but also with some common sense and logic.

The Nightmare

Nothing was easy on the army's journey. The Atlantic crossing took months. On arrival Braddock, his officers and the Forty-fourth and Forty-eighth Regiments of Foot found their priorities were not the priorities of the Virginians. The two-foot-wide path was difficult to turn into a twelve-foot-wide road, especially when the lush tree canopy turned daylight into darkness for much of the day. Moving the cannon up the slopes of a steep mountain and back down the other side was formidable. There were swamps. There were snakes. Indians hid behind trees and shot arrows at the column. Many of the men, including Braddock, believed they would never return to England. They were sure they would die in this wilderness. Archer Butler Hulbert reported in his book *Braddock Road and Three Relative Papers*: "Before we parted the General told me that he should never see me more; for he was going with a handful of men to conquer whole nations' and to do this they must cut their way through unknown woods. He produced a map of the country, saying, at the same time, 'Dear Pop, we are sent like sacrifices to the altar.'"[1]

For a little over the 120 miles from Fort Cumberland (Wills Creek) in Maryland to the town that now bears the general's name along the Monongahela River, the British, their American counterparts, wagoners (including Daniel Boone), women and a few Native Americans endured a nightmare that ended for most only in death. Those who survived the battle had to retreat back along the newly built road, carrying the wounded with them. Many more died. From start to finish, it was a disaster.

Finding the Road

One of the reasons we struggle to identify the route in Pennsylvania is that shortly after the ill-fated army made its way north, a shorter route to the Monongahela River became popular. That route, which eventually became the National Road, parted with the original near Jumonville and, instead of going north to the Monongahela near Pittsburgh, cut west down the mountain following a portion of Burd's Road to the river, where present-day Brownsville stands. That left the northern portion of Braddock Road in Fayette and Westmoreland Counties off the major trail west. One thing that helped preserve the route is that portions of Braddock Road became the border between townships. Today, of the eighty-five or so miles of Braddock Road in Pennsylvania, only traces can be found.

To be sure that the route will not be lost again, several groups are attempting to mark the road through their area. The first is the Braddock Road Preservation Association. Working out of Jumonville, they have erected signage to mark the road through their property and hold an annual seminar about the road. The concept and the use of signage was picked up by the Mount Pleasant Area Historical Society and the borough of Mount Pleasant and surrounding townships, which are trying to do the same thing for a six mile stretch of the road. As a beginning, the historical society held a seminar and brought together both historians and local people with knowledge of the road. In recent times, James Steeley, while serving as director of the Westmoreland County Historical Society, traced the road. Westmoreland Heritage published a guide based on Steeley's work. Fort Necessity received a grant from the National Park Service's American Battlefield Protection Program in 2002 to record the road through Fayette County using GPS and other modern equipment. The newest study has been done by Norman Baker, historian of the French and Indian War Foundation and a director of the Braddock Road Preservation Association. Norman, who considers his work definitive, has spent years walking the road, studying land grants and looking at it from an engineering point of view. His book *Braddock's Road: Mapping the British Expedition from Alexandria to the Monongahela* was published in 2013.

The general route in the Connellsville to Mount Pleasant area (the world of H.C. Frick) is clear. After crossing the Youghiogheny River at Connellsville, Braddock Road continues north through an area called the Narrows to the current Greenlick Lake. Here is the Great Swamp Camp. After stopping for rest, the army continued north, crossing Jacob's Creek and cutting through what is now fields along the township line between Mount Pleasant and East Huntingdon Townships to State Route 819. It reaches 819 around Bessemer Road. Cutting through Mount Pleasant more or less on Eagle Street, it arrives at the crossroads of Main Street (Route 31—Glade's Path) and Braddock Road Avenue and continues out of the borough via Sand Hill Road to Route 119 and the Industrial Park. It works its way through the Industrial Park and continues north to the Monongahela River.

That's the general route, although there are many contradictions along the way. Some are inconsequential. One is paramount: the route of Braddock Road changed over the years it was in use. What looks like a trace of Braddock's army could be a trace from a later portion of the road. Here we will discuss only two issues: the location of Jacob's Cabins and the crossing of the Youghiogheny at Connellsville. Both are important issues, for without finalizing them, the route will never be correct.

Jacob's Cabin Is Where?

Four modern accounts offer four different views of the location of Jacob's Cabin(s). Who was Jacob? He was a Delaware (Lenape) chief called Tewea who lived in the area before the influx of the Europeans. Jacob's Creek is named after him. One source maintains that Jacob's Cabin(s) was near the swamp, a second that a cabin was atop the hill on Sand Hill Road just above the berry farm. A third takes Jacob and his cabin well into the eastern section of the Industrial Park, a few miles beyond the Sand Hill area where another swamp existed. A fourth puts a cabin at the source of Jacob's Creek, farther south up the mountain. (Then, of course, there was another cabin belonging to Tewea at Kittanning where, a year after Braddock was killed, Tewea was killed at the Battle of Kittanning. His "cabin" was burned.)

These decisions as to the location of Jacob's Cabin(s) were mostly based on early journals and letters. Robert Orme, *Aid-de-camp* for General Braddock, wrote, "On the first of July, we marched about five miles, but could advance no further by reason of a great swamp which required much work to make it passable." This is Greenlick Lake, or the Great Swamp Camp. Then he reported, "On the 2nd of July, we marched to Jacob's cabin [sic] about 6 miles from the camp." Six miles from Greenlick along modern roads but following closely the direction of the army appears to be the top of Sand Hill Road, just beyond Mount Pleasant Borough. Orme goes on, "July 3rd. The swamp being repaired, we marched about six miles to the Salt Lick Creek."[2] The key here is "the swamp being repaired." I do not believe he is talking about the Great Swamp at Greenlick. In the Industrial Park north of Mount Pleasant borough, there is an additional swamp. Six miles, the usual effort for this army, will take one out of the Industrial Park and into Hunker and the Salt Lick, where modern scholars believe the Salt Lick Camp was located.

John Kennedy Lacock, a Harvard professor who walked and mapped the road in the early part of the twentieth century and believed he had found the road makes two points:

> *The preceding stop* [Great Swamp Camp] *was then a bivouac, not a camp. The camp referred to was the encampment one mile on the east side of the Xoughiogheny, at Stewart's Crossing. This day's march would be about one mile, and the place of encampment Jacob's Cabins. The two halting places were evidently both on the east side of Jacob's Creek. What is commonly known as the Great Swamp Camp was only the bivouac to which reference has been made…*
>
> *On the night of July 1 the army seems to have bivouacked in order that a swamp which existed for a considerable distance on either side of Jacob's Creek might be made passable. From the Truxell farm the line turns almost due north through the swamp crossing Green Lick Run, and thence keeping a straight line west of the Fairview church to a point a short distance west*

of Hammondville. Here, at a place called Jacob's Cabin [sic], *still on the east side of Jacob's Creek, the army encamped.*[3]

By most modern scholars, Lacock was wrong. The question remains: Six miles from what? From Stewart's puts the cabin or cabins just north of Greenlick but south of Jacob's Creek. Six miles from Greenlick puts the cabin or cabins atop Sand Hill or atop a hill within the Industrial Park area.

Then there is the account of George Fry Lee in his 1999 book *Westmoreland County History from a Mount Pleasant Township Perspective.* Lee states, "An Indian named Captain Jacobs by the white people, lived along the headwaters along the stream that bears his name, Jacob's Creek. His cabins were above the Mennonite camp…"[4]

Finally, in 1963, Paul A. Wallace reviewed the locations of the camps from July 1 to July 7. Using Gist's journals, reports of Captain Robert Cholmley's batman (servant) and Colonel Sir Peter Hackett's orderly book, all in *Braddock Road and Three Relative Papers*, he presents the idea that:

> *Jacobs Cabin was five or six miles beyond the camp at Green Lick Run— is reinforced by a warrantee survey showing a plot of land described as "a Mile and an half from Jacobs Hunting Cabbin* [sic] *on Braddocks road." Enough of the surrounding country, together with the road, is shown to pinpoint "the place where," as the surveyor has written on the drafts, "Jacobs Hunting Cabbin is said to have stood." Since he marked and described features of the landscape which are still easily identifiable, it is not difficult today to locate pretty closely the site of the cabin. It was on a gentle ridge just east of what was once Jacobs Swamp (since drained) and on or near a still passable road about two and a quarter miles north of the head of Eagle Street (the Braddock Road) in Mount Pleasant. In other words, Jacobs Cabin was five and a half miles, by the Braddock Road, from the crossing of Green Lick Run.*[5]

This supports Norman Baker's findings. In his book, Baker maintains Jacobs Cabin is on the hill in the Industrial Park, about a mile beyond Sand Hill.[6]

One possible explanation for all of these locations is that Chief Jacob had not one, but a number of cabins. He had a main cabin high on the mountain at the source of Jacob's Creek, above the modern Laurelville Mennonite Church Center, and he had a cabin at each of his hunting spots in our area. The truth is we can guess forever, we can quote from land grants and early publications, or we can do a good archaeological hunt and perhaps find the remnants of some of these cabins. Combined with current research, we may reach a consensus.

Crossing the Youghiogheny River

Perhaps the most controversial route of the army in our area is the crossing of the Youghiogheny River at Connellsville. Most contemporary accounts merely give the crossing a sentence. Therefore, one assumes that the crossing went smoothly enough that it was not noted. Lacock claimed: "Braddock forded the Youghiogheny at Stewart's Crossing, below the mouth of Opossum Creek, to a point on the opposite side of the river above the mouth of Mounts Creek, half a mile below Connellsville."[7] Lacock is following the words that appear in almost every journal.

Robert Orme reported the crossing, "on the 30th of June he reached Stewart's Crossing on the Youghiogheny, about thirty-five miles from his destination." Orme gave one of the most detailed reports on the crossing in his journal:

> *June the 30th. We crossed the main body of the Yoxhio Geni, which was about two hundred yards broad and about three feet deep. The advanced guard passed, and took post on the other side, till our Artillery and baggage got over; which was followed by four hundred men who remained on the east side 'till all the baggage had passed.*
>
> *We were obliged to encamp about a mile on the west side, where we halted a day to cut a passage over a mountain. This day's march did not exceed two miles.[8]*

Local Braddock Road enthusiasts do not believe the crossing was at Stewart's. They say, look across the river, what do you see? You see an almost sheer cliff. How could the army possibly climb that cliff with horses, cannon and supplies? They could not. Furthermore, the Broad Ford believers lament that the bed of the river was too rocky and too swampy to cross at Stewart's. There were copperheads. Men would sink into the mud up to their waists. Why endure all these hardships when a few miles lower (perhaps Lacock's "half a mile below Connellsville.") was an excellent crossing: Broad Ford. The name Broad Ford, found on a number of maps along several southwestern Pennsylvania streams, was given to sites used by the natives to show where they crossed.

One can justify Orme's "We were obliged to encamp about a mile on the west side, where we halted a day to cut a passage over a mountain." When crossing at Broad Ford, one does enter a small valley, and to reach the high ground, which is the way Braddock preferred to travel, one had and has to climb.

Brian Reedy, a ranger at Fort Necessity National Battlefield, who conducted the 2002 study to map Braddock Road through Fayette County, believes that the location of the crossing is now being questioned. He suggests that the army did cross below Stewart's, but above Broad Ford.

The Fort Necessity study mapped the road only in Fayette County. They concluded that most of the route runs through private property and therefore did not publish it. But they have the information and it is accessible through their offices.

The same type of study needs to be done in Westmoreland County. Yes, we really need to protect the rights of property owners (they in turn need to be stewards of the road), but we need to record the route of Braddock Road with modern tools like GPS and GIS. We also need archaeological work to support the research of men like Steeley and Baker. The litter of cannon balls, horseshoes, guns, buttons and boots may be the final word about the road. They surely litter the path of a flying army of two thousand men and thousands of horses. Braddock Road, one of the most important historical sites of the French and Indian War, needs to be celebrated.

THE NATIONAL ROAD IS NOT ROUTE 40

The National Road is not Route 40! Got it? Let me say it again: The National Road is not Route 40. If you don't listen to me, you will miss three-fourths of the glory of "America's first highway."

Now, let's get started. Although the National Road really originates in Baltimore, our journey begins in Pennsylvania's Laurel Highlands. That's mountain country, and it *ain't* easy going up and down the hills and vales, at least not for the pioneers. Therein lies the answer to the riddle.

Horses, cows and other animals could not pull wagons and stagecoaches straight up a hill, they had to go slowly up by a method called switchbacking. In other words, they would try to find the easy way by swinging to the left and then to the right in great *S*'s of slow incline. That is what the pioneers did.

That is what the National Road did, both up and down hills and mountains. On the other hand, cars can travel in a straight line up a hill and down a hill. So, Route 40 goes straight up and down. In doing so, it cuts off many exciting portions of the National Road.

"How did they find the route in the first place?" you might ask. Mountains have passes. The Alleghenies were no different. The animals found them first. Ten thousand strong—yes, ten thousand strong—the squirrels would race up and over and through and beyond. They would eat every inch of the way, encountering other migrating animals along the twisting and turning route, leaving the landscape fairly barren.

So, you can travel Route 40 if you want. I'm not. I'm going to follow the animals and the Native Americans who learned the routes from the wild beasts. I am going to keep my GPS glued to the old National Road.

If you stay on 40 as you descend Winding Ridge in what is now Somerset County, you are going to miss the charming and ancient village of Addison. It is the first stop in Pennsylvania, and it has the very first tollhouse, intact, maintained and open for visitors. By staying on 40 you will not sit with me under one of the trees and try to imagine all the animals passing the tollhouse "on the hoof" being assessed a fee—twenty sheep, six cents; twenty cattle, twelve cents; and forty hogs, six cents. Just envision the drovers trying to keep five thousand walking (and gaggling) geese from running away. The fees are still tacked on the tollhouse wall. It would be a pity to miss such a sight.

I will catch up to you on the other side of Addison, and we will both cross the new bridge over the Yough Dam Lake. When we do, neither of us will see the town of Somerfield now submerged beneath the lake. In 1936, the U.S. Army Corps of Engineers created the lake after the Saint Patrick's Day Flood decimated the region and created havoc in Pittsburgh. If we are lucky, the lake will be very, very, very low, and we will be able to see the Great Crossing Bridge, one of the finest stone bridges ever built along the National Road. This is where George Washington crossed the Youghiogheny River on November 18, 1753, and again when he led General Braddock and his army on June 24, 1755. Yes, our friend George led the way. On his first journey, Washington was led by a Native American chief called Nemacolin. The route became known as Nemacolin Path and a large portion was followed by the National Road. (In Washington County, the National Road followed Mingo Path, another Native American route.)

Now you can sit beside me as we watch Braddock and his two thousand men cross the river. See if you can pick out Daniel Boone. He was a teamster and would be driving one of the three hundred wagons that carried 200,000

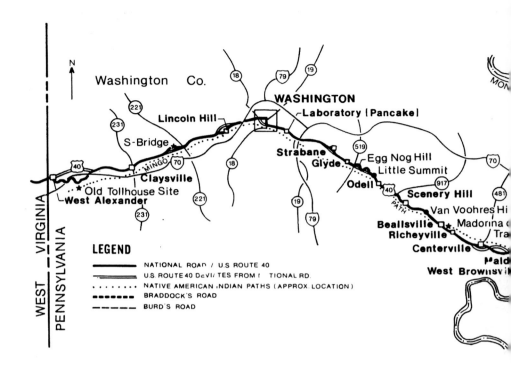

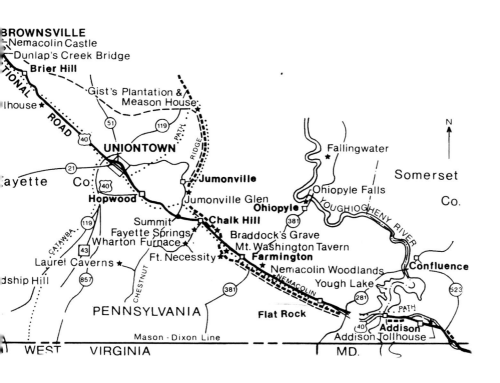

A map of the National Road from Addison to Brownsville including Braddock Road. *Courtesy of Yarris.*

Modern day re-enactors passing the Petersburg Tollhouse at Addison on National Pike Days. *Author's photo.*

pounds of flour, 10,000 sand bags, 400 spades and 4 eight-inch howitzers (it was an army after all). I doubt if you can recognize Christopher Gist, or Thomas Cresap, or George Croghan. I wouldn't recognize any of them either, but they were true pioneering men of the Laurel Highlands. Don't be surprised when you see the women. Yes, there were fifty women on this journey. Some were cooks and nurses. Others were wives.

We have to move quickly now because the four-mile-long column took quite a while to pass by. As we go up the hill and pass Browns Tavern, still standing in its magnificent two-story, cut-stone glory, we enter an area very popular during the Automobile Era of the National Road.*

There we encounter log cabin resorts and good ol' down-home restaurants, not to mention Nemacolin Woodland, our modern, ultra-chic resort. Braddock Road is running to our left, so neither of us will see Twelve

---

* The history of the National Road is broken into several eras: National Road Era (1811–1835); Toll Road Era (1835–1905); Automobile Era (1905–1996); and National Road Heritage Corridor (1996–present).

Springs Camp where General Braddock set up his eighth camp on June 24, 1755. The springs stand behind Shaw Tavern, a still-standing but rather derelict building. The springs are still there.

Once we reach the top of the mountain, there is very little room to roam to the right or to the left. As we approach Fort Necessity and the Great Meadow where Washington met his defeat at the guns of the French and Indians, Braddock Road still lies to our left. It is at the old Braddock Inn where it is believed Braddock was buried in the middle of the road that the two roads cross. A tollhouse once stood here too. The Vermont granite monument to Braddock is on our right.

I am not going to follow Braddock's Road off into the woods on our right. We will meet up with it at the crest of Chestnut Ridge. If you want to go, go ahead, but you will miss the National Road again.

Come along. Look to your left. Standing at the crest of Chestnut Ridge, in all of its magnificence, is the Spanish mission–style Summit Inn. They say that, on a clear day, you can see the Golden Triangle in downtown Pittsburgh from its grand veranda. That is over fifty miles away. It's a great place to stop for a cool drink and enjoy the view.

Directly across the National Road from the inn is the narrow road that leads to Rock Fort Camp, where Braddock and his men camped on June 28, 1755. Now we can take the short detour we did not take a few miles back. Awaiting us are Jumonville Glen and Dunbar's Camp, where Braddock's Army split: part remained here with the heavy baggage, while the general took a flying column and headed toward Fort DuQuesne (Pittsburgh). That means the National Road, which continues west, parts company with Braddock Road, which continues north.

I suppose you know what happened to the general and his men. Braddock expected to meet the enemy on the battlefield and fight in straight rows and columns, as it was done in Europe. He was not prepared to fight behind trees and bushes, guerrilla-style. He began to lose many men. Then he got shot. Some say by one of his own men, but we will leave that piece of hidden history for others to decipher. It is time for us to quench our thirst.

Be it on horseback or in a 1930s car, halfway up or down the mountain, a stop was necessary. So, there is the wonderful Water Trough on the mountain. The spring still gushes fresh, clear, mountain water, and I, for one, expect to imbibe. If you want your old bottled water, go ahead, not me.

At the very bottom of Chestnut Hill is the village of Hopwood. If you stick to Route 40 you will miss it, too, because 40 goes around the town while the National Road cuts through its heart. If there is one place you must stop

to visit it is Hopwood. Called the "Pearl of the Pike," it has no less than five extant Federal-style colonial stone buildings. I don't mind a pause to look around but not too long, for just beyond we can take a look at how the road was built.

This might be a good time for us to conjure up the men who built the road. They built it stone by stone. The Army Corps of Engineers surveyed it. Contracts were given to local companies along the road. It had a thirty-two-foot bed and a twenty-foot stone path. The stone had to be very smooth or the horses would have a hard time of it, and the wheels would fall off the wagons and stagecoaches all too often. When six hundred men of Braddock's army began building their road, they had to chop down trees, dig out the roots and level the ground. The men of the National Road had to do the same thing. Both used shovels, not bulldozers. Neither could use dynamite to blow up rocks because it was yet to be invented. Braddock's Road remained dirt, but not the National Road. But we cannot tarry, or they will put us to work. And that is hard work I don't want to do.

Next stop, Uniontown. Ironically, the National Road and 40 run in tandem through Uniontown past the old courthouse and jail, but if you want to see the old mansions of the great coal and coke era, you must turn left and left again to ride 40 East back to the end of Uniontown. Yes, 40 is a one-way street, and its two parts run parallel in Uniontown. The real National Road runs past the incredible courthouse building and jail. As we reach the end of town and turn west, heading toward Brownsville on the National Road, we pass the Trinity United Presbyterian Church with its bevy of Tiffany windows.

We can travel together along the next and very exciting section of the National Road between Uniontown and Brownsville. There is a tavern-a-mile along this route, and I challenge you to find them. They are not hard to spot. They have tin roofs. A few are the Moxley House, Josiah Frost House, Green Tree Tavern, Hatfield Tavern, Peter Colley Tavern, Skeen-Wallace Tavern, Red Tavern, Wilkes Brown Tavern and the Stone Home. There is even an old gasoline station, now a home, but it's easy to find, maybe.

Opposite, top: The water trough halfway up Chestnut Ridge in the early days of the National Road. *Courtesy of the author.*

Opposite, bottom: Searight's Tollhouse and toll keeper family, in the late 1800s. *Courtesy of the author.*

There is also one of the six Pennsylvania tollhouses—Searight's Tollhouse, built in 1835 of brick, not of stone. The mountains had stone tollhouses while the valley had brick. These two-story, six-sided brick buildings run all the way to the end of Pennsylvania in Washington County. This tollhouse, which was dynamited during the coal and coke era, was restored in 1966 and, like the Addison tollhouse, is open if we want to go inside.

Quite impressive isn't it? All this old stuff still here along the road? To me, it is wonderful. It is living history. Are you ready for more? Let's stop at the Peter Colley Tavern and sit on the porch to watch the early travelers go by. The Colley was one of the less-elegant taverns, but it still had good food and plenty of space in the back for the livestock to feed and rest (yes all those gaggling geese and grunting hogs). If we stay over, we will have to share a bed—not a room, a bed. And we might have to share it with two other strangers. Yes, four to a bed. That was the rule in pioneering days. Over 200,000 travelers a year walked or rode the National Road. They traveled in all kinds of weather: sleet, snow and blistering heat.

We can be sure to have a good meal of johnny cakes with maple syrup, oysters from Baltimore, fried squirrel and even venison (that's not only deer but other horned animals as well). But we will have to "mind our p's and q's" as we imbibe in Monongahela Rye and a little Bordeaux, claret, sauterne, sherry or cognac.

Oh, you don't know what your p's and q's are? When the travelers had settled in for the night and began having drinks, the bartender would watch how many pints and quarts they drank and would not let them have too many. Thus, "mind your p's and q's."

Now, on this porch we can watch the parade. First in view is a stagecoach. It might look funny, but it is really quite elegant. The interior is silk. The seats have cushions. It would cost $2.25 if we wanted to go from Uniontown to Washington, Pennsylvania. Who's inside? Henry Clay would ride the road on his way from Kentucky to Washington D.C. to attend Congress. If he is in there, we have to hide, for he would often get out and stand on a stump and talk for hours. We do not have hours.

Maybe it's Albert Gallatin? He is a local boy living down in New Geneva at the corner of the Highlands. He built the first glass factory west of the Alleghenies. He also was a driving force behind the National Road as he was United States Treasurer.

I would like to run into old Tom Searight. He was the great man of the road. He wrote a book called *The Old Pike* and is buried beside the road he loved so well. He believed there was never such a road, nor would there ever be one again. I would really like to meet old Tom.

Oh, look back there. Here comes a teamster. They carried everything: salt, flour, cotton, glass, tobacco, nails, guns, utensils, farm implements, logs for the iron furnaces that dotted the landscape, grain for distillers to turn into Overholt whiskey and Monongahela Rye (or Pure Mountain Dew, a highly prized moonshine). Look for the bells. Are any missing? If a driver gets into trouble and someone helps him he must give the good Samaritan one of his bells. They travel fast. They have deadlines. Be careful they do not run you down. If the road is blocked, they will run through the fields.

Gee, who was that zooming by? Did you see him? Bet it was a Pony Express rider. Yes, that's right. Before the Pony Express ran in the Wild West, the United States Post Office began running riders here on the National Road. There's lots of hidden history here. He sure left us in the dust. But we have got to move on. We are almost finished with our journey, for Brownsville is at the very edge of the Laurel Highlands.

You will miss the important town of Brownsville, if you ride 40 across the Monongahela River. You must, yes you must, turn right off 40 just before the Lane Bane Bridge, drive under it down Market Street, through an area called "the neck," cross the bridge and race up the other side of the river all the way to Maldin Inn. All of these wonders are *not* on 40. Are you getting the picture?

Brownsville was a hub of activity on the National Road. It was so important, it was once said, "Pittsburgh might amount to something if it weren't so close to Brownsville." We must stop. We cannot miss Nemacolin Castle, the Flat Iron Building, the oldest commercial district west of the Alleghenies, the first cast iron bridge in America, the first parish in Fayette County, the oldest church in Western Pennsylvania and the commercial and transportation center of the Klondike coal and coke fields of southwestern Pennsylvania? No, you do not want to miss Brownsville. In fact, I don't mind if we end our journey here. You can take your time and visit all the sites there are to see while I go visit some friends at the Transportation Museum (yes, another wonder in Brownsville).

I want to talk about all the boats built in Brownsville through the centuries. Yes, boats. From flat boats to keel boats, you could trade in your Conestoga for a boat to continue your journey west. Once you were on the river, you could sail north to Pittsburgh (you do know the Monongahela River flows north, don't you?), join the Ohio, float on to the Mississippi and journey south to New Orleans. Maybe you might want to stop at Saint Louis and get another wagon so you can move west. Up to you.

When they invented steam, Brownsville and its sister communities of California, Belle Vernon and Monongahela became steamboat builders. They made most of the steamboats that traveled west, that were in the Civil War and that moved the products of the Laurel Highlands to the rest of the country. But that is another story for another time.

The National Road continues across the river and into Washington County. The story is just as exciting, but I am not going to tell it here. That, too, is for another time. What I do want to say is that you have just traveled mile by mile down one of the most important roads in America. I will end with a quote by Tom Searight, whose ghost owns this road more than that of any other person. He "saw it in the zenith of its glory, and with emotions of sadness witnessed its decline." He shouted out for the world to hear that the National Road "was a highway at once so grand and imposing, an artery, so largely instrumental in promoting the early growth and development of our country's wonderful resources, so influential in strengthening the bonds of the American Union, and at the same time so replete with important events and interesting incidents." The National Road was the road of roads!

No Banks! No Credit Cards! Lots of Need!

So, how did the pioneers and the early immigrants buy what they needed? They bartered. The doctor delivered the new baby and went home with two chickens. Mary made a nice shawl and traded it in for eggs, butter, flour, salt and sugar. Little Bobby caught two fish and gave them to Mrs. Jones for a freshly baked apple pie, which he dutifully sat down and ate to the last crumb. That's how they did it.

Even if they did have some cash, there was no safe place to keep it. A pioneer in a Conestoga might put the money in the flour barrel. A homesteader in a log cabin might hide money in the barn under the hay. Others went out into the woods to find a safe place. Trouble is, barns burned and men died before telling anyone where the family wealth was kept. So, small family fortunes are still lying about in tree trunks, old wells, under rocks and all sorts of places.

People all over the world faced and still face these problems. In desert countries, even today, money is sometimes hidden in sand dunes, but more often, it adorns the family females in the form of gold or silver jewelry. In the Sudan, the Rashida women wear nearly one hundred pounds of silver

A Rashida woman in the Sudan wearing her family's wealth. *Author's photo.*

jewelry on their bodies. They put it on their heads, in their ears, through their noses, around their necks, on both wrists, on every finger and even on their ankles. Why do the women wear the wealth and not the men? Women stay home, so the wealth is safe. When funds are needed one of the bangles is taken and bartered for what is needed.

In the age of hard currency, poor people around the world still have a system to get what they need. They can't go to banks because they have no collateral. They do not have credit cards because their credit is bad. But their friends trust them, and their friends are just as needy as they are. So, they create their own temporary bank. It is done all over the world and is very simple.

Let's say I want to buy a new tablet but cannot save the $500 I need for the high-end version. I ask nine friends to join my bank. They agree to pitch in $50 a month for ten months. Then, each month one of the ten gets the $500. No interest. No fear of rejection. Because I started the club, I am the first one to get the $500 and by plunking down $50, my dream is realized. Next month, another happy member gets his or her dream come true.

A tablet is not a "must have," but stoves, refrigerators, hot water tanks and car tires and repairs certainly are. Even hospital visits require money. The bank also doesn't have to be $50. It could be $75, or even $25. Of course, all ten of the friends must remain friends by seeing the temporary bank through to the end.

THE MINE DISASTERS OF THE LAUREL HIGHLANDS

If you were asked to name one job you would never do, coal mining would probably be at the top of the list. Even today, walking into a dark tunnel is daunting, but at the beginning of the twentieth century, when coal mining was at its zenith in the Laurel Highlands and mining safety was at its nadir, mining was a nightmare.

There were cave-ins when the slag over the miner's head came tumbling down. Another danger was flooding when either floodwater or groundwater filled the mine and blocked all the entrances. The biggest threats of all were the gases, all kinds of them. They were invisible. Some gasses had no smell. Miners brought canaries into the mines just to check the gas levels. If the

The restored entrance to the Mammoth Mine No. 1 with monument on left. *Author's photo.*

canary dropped dead, everyone left the mine. The open-air flames on miner's lamps often caused explosions when they encountered gases. Miners wore them on their helmets to help see, as the mines were black as night.

Over 100,000 people have been killed in mining disasters in the United States since 1890. 1907 was one of the worse years, and 3,700 men and boys were killed during that year alone. Some of the greatest mining disasters the world has ever known happened in the Laurel Highlands. Here are a few of the major disasters.

Hill Farm Mine 1890

One of the earliest mass disasters in our region was in the tiny town of Dunbar, just off Route 119 in Fayette County. The catastrophe happened in June 1890. When workers tried to open a new borehole into the Hill Farm Mine, owned by the Dunbar Furnace Company, the mine exploded.

Hill Farm was an old mine by industry standards, having been established in the 1860s. The mine had about 150 beehive coke ovens to make the coke that the company used in their blast furnaces in Dunbar. It closed for good sometime in the 1920s. All that remains are six of the beehive ovens. They are believed to be the oldest beehives remaining in the region, but the few from the Mullen/Star mines outside of Mount Pleasant may prove them wrong.

The mine had been plagued by flooding and bad air for quite some time, and the bore would allow fresh air to enter. When miners attempted to penetrate into the wall of the bore, water began to gush, and the bore began to fill with gases. A young miner's lamp flame sparked the foul air, and a fire started. It was fueled by a brattice cloth used to line the borehole. The flames flew up the bore and fueled a pile of lumber and a barrel of pit car oil. At that point, the fire was out of control and could not be stopped.

The men were suffocated, and thirty-one of the fifty-seven miners in the mine at the time were trapped and died horrible deaths. Only two of the bodies could be retrieved as the fire was spreading. When rescue seemed impossible, the mine was sealed in order to put out the fire. It took two years for the fire to diminish. The mine was reopened in April of 1892 and the remaining twenty-nine men and children were found.

As a result of this accident, a new state law was adopted forbidding the tapping of a bore hole while men were in a mine. In September of 2011, over one hundred years after this tragedy, the miners were finally recognized with a ceremony and plaque erected in Dunbar.

Mammoth No. 1, 1891

On January 27, 1891, a firedamp explosion killed 109 (some say 116) miners at the H.C. Frick Coke Company's Mammoth No. 1 Mine along Sewickley Creek at Route 982 in Westmoreland County. It was opened in 1886 by the Colonel J.W. Moore Coke Company of Greensburg and sold to the H.C. Frick Coke Company in 1889. After having closed the mines and ovens in 1927, Frick leased the coke works to developers John Dent and Gus Kelly in the 1930s. They operated it until 1946, when it was sold and strip-mined. Mammoth was one of the largest mines at the time, and in addition to the mine, there were five hundred coke ovens.

The newspapers reported that when the explosion occurred, black vapor spewed from the top of the 107-foot shaft. There were 109 miners in the mine, and all 109 were killed. The company began an extensive safety campaign because of this tragedy, which was then enforced in all Frick mines. The mine was reopened a year later.

Most of the men and boys, unidentifiable because of the intensity of the explosion, are buried en masse at Saint John the Baptist Cemetery, south of Scottdale along Route 819. A Pennsylvania Historical Marker was erected at the cemetery in 2002.

Today, the extant boiler house houses the Mount Pleasant Township Supervisors office, and the grounds are used to store equipment. In tribute to the miners, the entrance to the mine has been rebuilt and a monument erected to honor those who perished in the mine. Unfortunately, of the 311 coke ovens at No. 1, none remain. Many were destroyed as late as 1993. A few were placed in nearby Mammoth Park.

The Worst Year: 1907

One of the worst years and months in coal mine disasters in not only the highlands but the entire United States was December 1907. Approximately 806 Pennsylvania miners lost their lives that year. The worst disaster in American history came on December 6, when the Monogah No. 6 and No. 8 mines in West Virginia, owned by the Fairmont Coal Company just outside of the highlands, exploded. Officially, 362 men and boys were listed as dead, but the toll is believed to be much higher. In the highlands, there were a number of catastrophes that month too; the two most devastating were at Naomi Mine in Fayette County and the Darr Mine in Westmoreland County.

Naomi Mine

On December 1, 1907, an explosion rocked the large Naomi Mine of the United Coal Company near Fayette City, Fayette County. The explosion was so intense, the shock could be felt a great distance, and it destroyed a few mine buildings nearby. The fire caused by the explosion raged so intensely that rescue parties could not enter the mine to look for the men trapped inside.

A spark from the electric lights, which had recently been installed in the mine, caused the explosion. However, poor ventilation was the major culprit. Ironically, the month before, the state inspectors had sent the owners a letter warning about the air quality in the mine. The miners were working almost a mile from the entrance, and rescue efforts were difficult. A few days later, twenty-four bodies were recovered; a few days after that, the number grew to thirty-two. By December 12, thirty-four bodies were accounted for. That was the final count.

Some of the miners were taken to the Mount Auburn Cemetery in Fayette City where a small plaque marks their grave. In November of the same year, the state inspectors had sent the owners a letter warning about the air quality in the mine. The Naomi mine was closed and some of the miners sought and got work at the Darr Mine in Rostraver Township. The Naomi Mine was purchased by Hillman Coal and Coke Company around 1920. The Hillman Company focused on mining coal with qualities not high enough for use in coke ovens, and much of their coal was shipped overseas. It owned twenty-three mines in the region.

Darr Mine

On December 19, 1907, the Darr Mine on the Youghiogheny River near the coal patch of Van Meter in Rostraver Township, Westmoreland County exploded in a combination of gas and dust, killing 239 miners. The Darr Mine was first opened in the 1850s, making it one of the first mines in the region. In 1907, it was owned by the Pittsburgh Coal Company, belonging to the Mellon family. In 1945, it merged with the Consolidation Coal Company (CONSOL), belonging to the Rockefeller family.

Miners lived in two patches: one near the mine in Van Meter and another across the river in Jacobs Creek. Originally, some of the miners would use a cable car ferry stretched across the Youghiogheny River to reach the mine from the coal patch of Jacobs Creek, but at some point, it was replaced by a swing bridge. Ironically, December 19 is Saint Nicholas Day for the

Carpatho-Rusyn community, and many of the Darr miners had taken the day off to attend mass and celebrate at the nearby Saint Nicholas Greek Church. The saint's day saved their lives. It has been called a miracle.

It is believed that open-flame miner's lamps might have caused the explosion. The mine had been gaseous for some time, and a new shaft had been dug. Sadly, it had yet to be joined to the mine to alleviate poor ventilation. Some of the miners are still interred at Darr, but seventy-one are buried in a mass grave at the Olive Branch Cemetery along Route 981, near Smithton. As was typical of the day, the owners, the Pittsburgh Coal Company, were exonerated.

Eventually the mine was reopened in 1910 as Banning No. 3 Mine. As part of Banning Three, it remained in operation until 1919. Like many mines, it had a short rebirth around 1950. No monument or marker honors the miners at the mine, although the location of the mine is noted along the Great Allegheny Passage Trail. In 1994, eighty-seven years after the event, a Pennsylvania Historic Marker was erected at the cemetery.

After the December 1907 fiascos, the industry fell under great scrutiny, and by 1910, the United States Bureau of Mines was created. Accidents diminished but were never wiped out. Mine disasters continue today. Among the most disastrous in the Laurel Highlands happened at the Gates Mine No. 2 in Gates when an explosion killed twenty-five men in February 1922. Gates No. 1 in Brownsville erupted in an explosion in July 1924, killing ten. In 1952, six miners were killed when the Carpentertown mine in Carpentertown, near Mount Pleasant, exploded.

One Great Victory

On July 24, 2002, the Quecreek Mine of the Black Wolf Coal Company in Somerset County began to fill with water. It happened when miners erroneously broke through to the nearby Saxman Mine. Saxman, which had been closed for decades, was above Quecreek Mine and filled with groundwater. Water often penetrates into the unused tunnels of mines. With the breach, the water began pouring into Quecreek, and eighteen miners were in danger of being trapped. Nine got out, but nine remained behind. They were 240 feet below ground.

The first step to save the miners was to drill a hole down to their location and pour in air to give them oxygen and push back the water. That was quite a challenge. First, the exact location had to be determined above ground.

They were below a farm owned by the Dormel family. Then rescuers had to decide just how they were going to drill this hole. They determined they needed a bore drill. They started to drill, but the drill bit cracked and they were back to where they had started. They had to start again, and it took over a day before the drill hole was finished. The rescuers tapped on the pipe to see if anyone would answer. Nine taps came back.

The work continued through a series of obstacles. So many things could go wrong. Breaking into the pocket could cause the water to rush in and drown the miners. The walls of the hole could collapse. They could break yet another drill bit. The miners were now breathing compressed air, and if brought out of the mine too fast, they could decompress (so hyperbaric chambers had to be brought). And on and on and on.

A second escape hole was started. That drill broke its bit. But finally, on the morning of July 27, three days after the disaster, Rescue Hole No. 1 broke into the mine. On July 28, the first of the nine miners was brought to the surface via a steel mesh escape capsule. Every fifteen minutes another miner reached the surface.

The United States Mine Safety and Health Administration determined that the reason for the disaster was an undated and uncertified mine map. It put the Saxman Mine in the wrong place. All mine maps in the country were to be updated, scanned and placed in the Department of Environmental Protection (DEP) offices for easy access. To honor the miners, Quecreek has erected a memorial park on the grounds.

As long as men go down into the mines, there will be tragedies. As Louis Untermeyer wrote in this poem *Caliban in the Coal Mine*:

> *Nothing but blackness above*
> *And nothing that moves but the cars…*
> *God, if You wish for our love,*
> *Fling us a handful of stars!*

LET'S DO SOMETHING ABOUT THE ABANDONED COKE OVENS

The best time to go coke-oven hunting is in the winter. You can see them lurking in various stages of decay in the woods along country roads. Sometimes there is only one. Sometimes there are two or three. Sometimes you hit the mother

Standard Coal Mine beehive coke ovens and slag dumb (gob pile). *Courtesy of the author.*

lode and find an entire row of ten or more. Coke ovens are a rich heritage that we have forgotten and allowed to be devoured by weeds.

Coke ovens were invented in China. The beehive kind came first and was called a beehive because it had a round top. During strikes, when the owners threw the men and their families out of the coal patches, some families went to live in the beehive coke ovens. But coke ovens evolved into squares, batteries and, today, uninteresting metal monsters.

So what is coke? Coke is cooked bituminous, or soft, coal. The coal is burned in the coke oven until it is almost as hard as a diamond and is nearly pure carbon. Then, it is sent to steel mills (and other factories) and burned in blast furnaces to make iron, which was fed into open-hearth furnaces to make steel and other products.

How many coke ovens are there in the Connellsville Coke Region? In May 1900, there were 20,263 coke ovens in the entire Connellsville Coke Region, which extended through most of the counties in southwestern Pennsylvania including Fayette, Somerset and Westmoreland. In fact, from 1882 to 1912, the height of the coke oven period, 71 percent of all coal mined in Pennsylvania was mined in the Connellsville Coke Region in eighty-nine different plants. Almost all were beehive ovens. Credit for the last beehive coke ovens to operate in Western Pennsylvania is always given to the Calumet Coke Works in Mount Pleasant Township. Those ovens were still working in the early 1970s. But the coke ovens at Alverton in East Huntingdon Township were often fired up as late as the 1980s.

So, what are we going to do with all these coke ovens? They are our heritage, after all. In fact, where are they? Where are the coal mines? Where are the entrances? Are they secured? It is clear that very few of the buildings, tipples and coke ovens of the great coke and coal industry of the Connellsville Coke Region remain. Few people know exactly where the mines were located, nor do they know the historical significance of the industry that built America. In addition, in a zeal to clear up pollution and maintain the natural world, the remnants of the industry are slowly being obliterated by well-meaning environmentalists: coke ovens are purposely being destroyed and gob piles (slag dumps) are intentionally being decimated.

Another option for environmentalists (and all of us) would be to salvage the portions of the coal industry that remain, clear the rubble and provide historical information about the sites. Maintaining sites in this manner will not only preserve some of what remains but contribute to the ongoing environmental cleanup begun in the 1920s.

One place where we can see the effects of such an effort is at the offices of the Mount Pleasant Township Supervisors along Route 981 in Mammoth, Pennsylvania. The supervisor's offices occupy one of the buildings of the abandoned Mammoth Mine. They have rebuilt the entrance to the mine and erected a memorial to the miners.

It would not be hard to implement such a project. All coal mines were along rural roads often built by the companies themselves. They are along railroad tracks also built to support the coal industry. Many of the railroads have been turned into hiking trails. So, just clearing the debris to make the coke ovens visible, maintaining the clearances and erecting signs indicating the names of the mines and a little history is all that is needed.

Of course, it all needs to be organized and properly done. Please, whatever you do: do not restore the ovens. Clean them up, yes. Pull the weeds and shrubs, clear the garbage and eliminate the threat of snakes and other vermin, yes. Maintain the ruins and find an environmental group who will volunteer on a regular basis to keep the area clear, yes. Restore the ruins, no! Stabilize them, but keep the coke ovens in ruins. People travel great distances to see ruins all over the world (Egypt, Rome, India, etc.) The coke ovens and remaining tipples are the ruins of our great industry.

Then what? The sky is the limit! Develop a local coke trail for automobiles and hikers. Link it to other trails. As mentioned, we still use the existing roadways (built by coal barons to service their coal mines). With the recent completion of the Great Allegheny Passage (GAP) which claims over eighty-thousand visitors and over $8 million a year in local wages, not only are our abandoned coke ovens great for tourism, they are important for economic development.

The H.C. Frick Coke Company at the 1893 Chicago World's Fair

The Chicago World's Fair opened its doors in May 1893. Dominating the Mines and Mining Exhibition Hall was a replica of the largest and most modern mine in the world. It wasn't in England. It wasn't in France. It wasn't even in Colorado. It was right here in Mount Pleasant Township, Westmoreland County. Let me repeat that. This mine was the leader of the world in mining coal, turning it into coke and using the most modern equipment and techniques to do it. Bar none, it was the best. That mine was the H.C. Frick Coke Company's Standard Shaft No. 2.*

An H.C. Frick Coke Company promotional image of its holdings in the Connellsville Coke Region. *Courtesy of the Library of Congress Digital Prints and Photographs Collection.*

---

* Standard had a number of mines and both No. 2 and No. 3 are mentioned by various sources as the model of this replica. No. 3 was not created until 1901, so No. 2 was the mine represented at the Chicago World's Fair.

The Company and the Mine

In the early 1870s, a young man from West Overton, named Henry Clay Frick, went to Pittsburgh to visit family friend Judge Mellon. Frick asked the judge for a loan of $10,000. Mellon liked his spunk and gave him the money. That was the beginning of Henry Clay Frick's empire. Frick built those first coke ovens on family property at Broad Ford, near the distillery which his family, the Overholt family, owned and operated, and along a portion of the old Braddock Road. Before his career was over, Frick would own hundreds of mines, making the Connellsville Coke Region the most famous industrial site in the world. At the time of the World's Fair in 1893, his company had forty-three plants producing 21,000 tons of coke a day, and 10,148 of the 17,000 coke ovens in the region.[9] It would grow well beyond those figures in the years ahead.

In 1886, seven years before the fair, Frick built Standard Shaft No. 2. Standard was the biggest and the best. Everyone knew it. From the lowliest miner in the smallest mine in the United States to the elite of the coal fields in Britain and Germany, Standard was the standard. Men came from around the world to see the how and why of Standard Shaft. They traipsed through it and observed its operations. The glory of the mine was its shaft. It was sunk to a depth of three hundred feet, right into the Pittsburgh Coal Seam. A shaft was like an elevator. It carried men and equipment into and out of the mine. This one was an engineering marvel. All the men, animals and equipment needed to mine the coal were lowered and raised from one of the shafts two cage ways, and all of the mined coal was raised the same way.

The mine operated well into the twentieth century. In the 1910s, it reached the height of coal production. But in 1931, during the Depression, United States Steel, which incorporated the Frick mines into its holdings, closed all three Standard mines. The patch houses and company store were sold. The mine machinery and animals were moved elsewhere. The mine was secured, and along with the coke ovens, it was abandoned. Now, nearly a century later, the red brick machine shop (built in 1885) and the hipped-roofed lamp house are still there. So are the patch houses that line both sides of Route 819. The company store still stands. The tipple is gone. The magnificent shaft, so famous a century ago, is gone. The mine itself still spreads out under houses, roads and fields. No one mines it anymore. It is probably filled with water. Most of the coke ovens that ran between the patches along the east side of 819 are gone. Only a few, covered with brush and trees and slowly decaying, remain as a tribute to "the greatest mine in the world."*

Preparing for the Fair

When Fredrick J.V. Skiff, director of the fair committee of the newly created Mines and Mining division, asked for mining submissions, West Overton–born Henry Clay Frick, "the greatest industrialist in the world," and fast becoming "the most hated man in America," asked for and got fifty square cubic feet of space.† His plan was to show the world how mining and coking was done in the Connellsville Coke Region. Frick chose Robert Ramsay to create the replica. Ramsay was one of three Mount Pleasant brothers who superintended Frick mines through the years. He invented the Ramsay Ram: an apparatus atop a tipple that would tilt rail cars to unload their coke. He had designed the original shaft at Standard. Now he was its superintendent and would duplicate the shaft to 1/25 its size.

Work began around March 1892, right on the grounds of Standard Shaft No. 2. It took six men a year to complete the entire replica. It was an amazing accomplishment. No expense was spared. No corners cut. First, they had to contour the land to resemble the topography of the area. Then they lay in the buildings, the rails and all the items related to the site. In the end, it cost the company $12,000 to produce.

The shaft was the most complicated building to create. When the miners went into the mine at Standard, they entered the shaft and walked into the cage way. The cage then descended into the mine where the men worked to extract the coal from the seam. In a single day, the four hundred men working in twelve-hour shifts would mine about two thousand tons of coal. The miners would hit the walls with picks until chunks of coal fell to the ground. Then they loaded the coal onto buggies, which were pulled by horses or mules to the bottom of the shaft. There, the coal was lifted up the

---

* It is believed that Frick erected less than 1,000 coke ovens because he would have to pay additional tax if he built 1,001. A Pennsylvania historic marker has been erected at Standard Shaft.

† While the replica was being built and preparations were underway to go to the fair, the great Homestead Strike of 1892 was waged. It showed Frick as a cold, calculating man who would go to great lengths to protect company interests against worker's demands.

A good view of the Standard Shaft No. 2 with the tipple on the left, the railroad cars beneath the tipple, the shaft apparatus above the tipple and various mine buildings surrounding it. *Courtesy of the Mount Pleasant Public Library.*

shaft via the cage way into the open air.* The buggies were then pushed onto tracks. All of this had to be illustrated on the replica. The coal was made of asbestos. The buggies, some called larrie or larry cars, had nickel-plated brass wheels. So did the bins, the pit wagons, the tracks (laid on wooden ties) and the railroad engines (built by Morris Ramsay, the nineteen-year-old son of Robert).

From the shaft, the coal was driven along tracks to the coke ovens. Around 320 men, called "cokers," dumped the coal into awaiting coke ovens (nine hundred plus of them) and fired them up to convert the coal into coke. It was this process that caused one traveler to say the region looked like "Hell with the lid off." In the replica, sixty-four working coke ovens were created of cast-iron. The illusion of burning coal was created by gas pumped into the ovens to create smoke. Once the coal was turned into coke, the coke was removed from the ovens, reloaded onto the larrie cars and sent to a tipple.

---

* These men would win and keep the world's daily record of hoisting coal up out of the shaft.

The tipple was the place where the coke was tipped into river barges or railroad cars. At Standard, the wooden tipple loomed over the railroad tracks of the B&O and the Southwestern Pennsylvania Railroads. The railroad cars would be pulled under the tipple. The larrie cars would loom overhead and, one by one, move into place and dump their loads into the railcars to be shipped to awaiting steel mills and other industries around the country. These actions were duplicated on the replica.

In addition to the shaft, the cast iron coke ovens, the wooden tipple, the tracks and the rolling stock of various kinds, the model included all the buildings of the mine: the boiler house; the blacksmith, carpenter and machine shops; and a few wooden workers' homes with front porches, interior furniture and backyard gardens.

Most of the men working on the replica had a specialization. James Wilson built the rams that pushed the cars onto and off of the hole in the tipple, where they would discharge the coke into the awaiting railroad cars. David Patterson and his assistants—Samuel Bungard, Elmer Billings and George Walters—constructed the wooden items like the tipple, the rail ties, the wagons and the houses. Billings and Walters made the bin and pit wagons too. Charley Fletcher, John Shindle, James Cox and Bert Bobbs were the painters. Their work included turning the solid red façades of several building into bricks. Patterson and Bungard took the replica to Chicago and reassembled the model at the fair. The *Mount Pleasant Journal* reported, "Everything about the model, except the electric lights, was made here… except the piston rods on the engines which are steel…the Westinghouse Company supplied the lights in keeping with the scale."[10]

On March 24, 1893, the work was completed, and the replica was put on view for the general public. Thousands came to see it. On that Sunday alone, nearly three thousand people passed by it.

Leisenring No. 2, Too!

Frick built Standard Shaft No. 2. He bought Leisenring No. 2 and its two sister mines from the Connellsville Coke and Coal Company in 1889–90. The Leisenring mine began operations in 1882. It had a deeper seam than Standard Shaft, and the shaft was built down to 500 feet (another source says 398 feet). According to the "Report of the Operation and Output of the Coke Ovens of the Connellsville Region for the week ending Saturday, May 21, 1892," which appeared weekly in the *Connellsville Courier*, Leisenring had

423 miners and cokers and 500 beehive coke ovens.[11] One of the reasons Frick added the Leisenring shaft to his replica was that it was built of steel, another first in the industry.[12]

When the mine slowly closed in the late 1950s, the shaft super structure was sent to the Maple Creek Mine, near Charleroi in Washington County. That mine did not close until the early 2000s. The steel super structure still stands.[13] As a visitor entered the Mine and Mining building, the Leisenring No. 2 shaft was the first thing to be seen.

Beyond the Replica

All around the perimeter of the display, Frick had additional items related to coke and coal. Near the Leisenring Shaft were five cars loaded with coke and a few more cars loaded with coal. Both were built to one-tenth of their size. There was also a pyramid built of coke, and near it, a series of glass bins with more coke that people could pick up and handle. Surrounding the exhibit were revolving stands with pictures of various mines of the H.C. Frick Coke Company. Three maps were placed around the display. The first was a topographical map of the Connellsville region (at a cost of $15,000). The second located the Frick mines of the region. Yet a third map illustrated the workings of the Leisenring Mine No. 3. Over the exhibit was a velvet

Some of the more than nine hundred coke ovens at Standard Shaft. In the foreground is Standard Patch, where the miners lived. *Courtesy of the Mount Pleasant Area Historical Society.*

thirty-two-foot-high sign reading: H.C. FRICK COKE CO. CONNELLSVILLE COKE. The letters were made of coke.

There was one more little Frick miracle: an elaborate pamphlet called *Connellsville Coke*. It described the process of mining coal and turning it into coke. There seems to have been two versions of this pamphlet: one to distribute to the masses and a second, with an embossed cover, either reserved for special guests or created out of the original pamphlet and the photographs in the exhibit and made a few years later.

What Happened to the Replica?

The Chicago World's Fair came to an end in 1893. When the time came to pack up the exhibits and take them home, Frick wrote to his General Manager Thomas Lynch, "I would not want the Chicago exhibit disturbed at all, even

The H.C. Frick Coke Company display at the World's Fair. Not everything is visible in this image of the replica and surrounding items. *Courtesy of the author.*

the models of the individual cars, until I have a full talk with you on the subject. My idea is to keep it intact, store it away somewhere, and use it for some future exhibition."[14] In November, the answer came, "I have decided to have our World's Fair exhibit removed to Exhibition building in this city, as it will be of great interest to many of our customers, when they happen to be in this city and avoid the necessity of them taking a trip to the coke region to see the operation of coke making."[15] And that is where it remained through 1894, 1895 and the Western Pennsylvania Exposition of 1898.

After that, the replica, or some of its parts, may have been exhibited in various fairs and expositions but eventually bits and pieces were placed in personal collections. For years, one of the cars was in the window of a bank in Uniontown.

Glass: A Major Industry in the Laurel Highlands

Glass! Amazing glass, beautiful glass! Glass is created where you throw a number of ugly, opaque substances together, liquefy them with intense heat and turn them into clear or colored, transparent or opaque, blemish-free, highly desirable items. Whether it is flat and clear and used as windows or delicate and patterned into myriad forms and uses, glass is an art form and a wonderful addition to our world.

Through the centuries, it took a team to make a single piece of glass. The workforce was divided into groups and each group would produce a specific glass pattern on any given day: one craftsman melted the glass and kept it molten; a second would take the small gobs of glass from the furnace to the work space; a third would blow, mold or press the glass into its basic shape. If the piece needed a stem, there was a man for that. If it needed a foot, another man did that task. It would not be outrageous to say that seven to nine men were needed to produce a single piece of stemware. They could create about 360 pieces of a specific pattern of glass a day. That was before automation. Where nine men were needed to make a single glass of a certain pattern, through automation, the team could be reduced to three men and production could be doubled or tripled.

Southwestern Pennsylvania is a major story in the history of glass. More plants existed here than anyplace else in early America. The industry spilled over to West Virginia and Ohio until the tri-state area was the most important

A glassblower and his team making glass at the Bryce Brothers factory in Mount Pleasant. *Courtesy of the Mount Pleasant Glass Museum.*

manufacturing center for glass, perhaps in the world. That dominance existed well into the late twentieth century. It is time we recognize glass for the major industry it was and celebrate it not only for its beauty and craftsmanship but for its economic impact on the region as well.

As early as 1797, the first glass was being manufactured in Fayette County. Soon to be a United States senator, Albert Gallatin in New Geneva owned one of those early factories. But there were dozens, if not hundreds, of small glass businesses in the region. Some lasted only a few years, but a few managed to stay alive for over a century and make an indelible mark on glass manufacturing. Two of the most famous centers for glass in Pennsylvania were at Jeannette (including Grapeville) and Mount Pleasant, both in the highlands.

Jeannette

Jeannette is a city that was founded on glass. It remained a glass center for over a hundred years and became known as Glass City, employing over 2,500 workers by 1918. If the truth be told, there were so many glass factories in Jeannette and they merged, combined, unmerged and recombined until it is so confusing that no two researchers tell the same history. Suffice to say, Jeannette *was* glass.

Two Pittsburgh men began it all: James Chambers and H. Sellers McKee. They formed a partnership called Chambers-McKee and moved their factories out of the cramped quarters of Pittsburgh to several sprawling farms and founded the community of Jeannette. As with the coal industry that was developing in the region, the two men created company houses and a company store. Chambers brought his Pittsburgh window-making plant to Jeannette while McKee established the McKee Glass Company and continued to make tableware. In Jeannette, they had all the natural gas they needed and enough space to develop integrated plants.

By 1899, Chambers consolidated his holdings in the region and created the American Window Glass Company. For nearly one hundred years, the manufacturing giant continued to produce window glass, but by the mid-1900s, things began to change. In the 1950s, it merged with Blue Ridge Glass and became known as American Saint-Gobain. In 1993, it closed for good.

In 1899, McKee sold his business to the National Glass Company tableware trust. It became the McKee-Jeannette Glass Company in 1904. *History of Westmoreland County*, written in 1906, claims that the first glass factory in Jeannette was the McKee-Jeannette Glass Works and called it the "largest tableware glass factory in the world," sending its wares throughout America and into Europe. The factory went through several transformations, including name changes, but continued to produce a variety of glassware, including pressed glass, jadite, white milk glass, black glass and Glasbake (similar to Pyrex). In 1917, they began manufacturing automobile headlight lenses. By 1951, McKee-Jeannette belonged to the Thatcher Glass Company, and ten years later, it was absorbed into the Jeannette Glass Company.

The Jeannette Glass Company also operated in the 1890s. It stood beside the McKee Glass Company. In the 1920s, it began making pressed ware. A recent publication on the community says the Jeannette Bottle Works was established in 1888. It made bottles and flasks. That included prescription bottles, bottles for beer and liquor companies and even milk bottles. It was absorbed into Jeannette Glass in 1898. A year after that, it began manufacturing glass jars for pickles, olives and mayonnaise. All of these companies closed in 1983. People who covet collecting this glass think nothing of digging into old, abandoned outhouses looking for the treasures. Once they find one, they can command prices in the thousands of dollars (or only a dollar).

Two other Jeannette companies were the Empire Glass Company, which began in 1904 and concentrated on making chimney glass, and the Fort Pitt Lamp, Brass and Glass Works. The former started as a mold company and, by 1910, became the Jeannette Shade and Novelty Company. The latter, like many, began in Pittsburgh. Around 1901, it opened the Jeannette factory and closed the Pittsburgh factory. Unlike Chambers and McKee, Fort Pitt produced a variety of glass items, both flint and opal. They included lamps, shades, stands, chimneys and lamp extras.

Today, a single glass company, the Jeannette Specialty Glass Company, remains in business in Jeannette. However, you can find Jeanette glassware in almost every garage sale and auction around the area. There are also several small clubs devoted to the glass made in Jeannette.

Grapeville

Near Jeannette, in a small town called Grapeville, stood the Westmoreland Specialty Company, founded in 1889. It was originally the Specialty Glass Company in Ohio. By 1924, its name was changed to the Westmoreland Glass Company. Westmoreland produced an enormous variety of glass in both pressed and cut forms. From little doggies to candy containers to nesting chickens, all in a variety of colors, Westmoreland Glass was prolific and wonderful. Then, beginning in the 1940s, it turned its attention and its line to milk glass.

By the 1980s, as the glass industry was fading, the company was sold to a Saint Louis businessman and resold a few years later. It closed for good in 1984.

A map of known glass factories in the 1960s. *Courtesy of the Mount Pleasant Glass Museum.*

Westmoreland Glass has a huge following around the country, and each spring, the National Westmoreland Glass Collector's Club has a convention in the area.

Mount Pleasant

Not too far southeast of Jeannette is the older town of Mount Pleasant. Mount Pleasant was a colonial town and played a major role in the development of early coal mines, coke ovens and a young man named Henry

Clay Frick. At the end of the nineteenth century, when coal was beginning to wane in the region, glass discovered the picturesque community. Mount Pleasant became home to three world-famous glass factories that operated for well over a century. Bryce Brothers, founded in 1850, came to the Mount Pleasant area in 1893, when it bought the Smith-Brudewold factory at Hammondville (another Mount Pleasant glass factory). In 1896, Bryce Brothers incorporated and moved to Depot Street in Mount Pleasant and remained there until 1965, when it was acquired by Lenox Crystal.

Unlike most the other glass factories in the region, Bryce Brothers glass was not pressed, it was blown. That made it superior. It was also crystal. Crystal is different. It has lead in it. That gives it its fine quality and separates it from other types of glass. Bryce Brothers was among the finest glass crystal manufacturers in the world, but is the least known. Unlike other glass factories, Bryce does not have a book, nor is there a club, and most people have trouble recognizing it. Now, however, it has a museum and a book is in the works.

Lenox

Lenox was founded by Walter Scott Lenox, in 1889, as the Lenox Ceramic Art Company. At its plant in New Jersey, it quickly gained a reputation for creating elegant china tableware, and through the years, in addition to gracing embassies around the world, its fine china was also on the tables of presidents Wilson, Roosevelt, Truman, Reagan, Clinton, Bush and Obama.

Lenox did not begin making hand-blown lead crystal until 1966, when it came to Mount Pleasant and bought Bryce Brothers Company. Its intention was to create crystal to match its tableware. In 1970, Lenox moved from the old Bryce factory on Depot Street in Mount Pleasant to a new plant on Route 31. At that time, 350 people worked for Lenox. As the market declined, Lenox dropped the Bryce line in favor of its own. The Brown-Forman Corporation purchased Lenox in 1983. Based in Louisville, Kentucky, its empire included Jack Daniel's Tennessee whiskey as well as Lenox and Gorham.

By the end of the twentieth century, the Lenox plant in Mount Pleasant was the only place in the United States producing hand-blown crystal stemware. Lenox began the long process of automation at its Mount Pleasant plant. However, by 2001, the American desire for fine crystal was in deep decline, while the plant was making more glass than it could possibly sell. At that time, the plant employed 158 people.

To add to the problem, the Environmental Protection Agency wanted Lenox to take the lead out of the glass. Lead was poisonous. It created health hazards for the workers. But try as they might, Lenox could not find the recipe to keep making quality glass without lead. So, they sent their production overseas (where leaded crystal is made and imported into the United States). It closed for good in January 2002.

L.E. Smith

Three men founded L.E. Smith Glass Company in 1902 : Louis E. Smith, Charles Walter and Thomas Edward Wible. They opened their first factory in Jeannette, but in a few years, they purchased the bankrupted Anchor Glass Company (yet another Mount Pleasant glass factory) and moved to Mount Pleasant. If the truth be told, L.E. Smith was not the moving and sustaining force behind this glass factory. All he wanted was to make glass jars for his Smith's German Mustard. He left the company by 1911. The Wible and Spence families and heirs kept the factory going for generations.

An L.E. Smith ad in the *New York Times*, February 21, 1960. *Courtesy of the Mount Pleasant Glass Museum.*

Among the famous L.E. Smith items are automobile headlight lenses, including the first one for the Ford Model T in 1917. Smith continued to make the lenses for Ford, Dodge and Lincoln as late as the 1940s. In the 1930s, they became the largest manufacturers of black glass in the country. They also invented the glass percolator top for coffeepots. In the 1960s, L.E. Smith made huge bittersweet vases, which were two feet and sometimes even three feet tall. The yellow-orange figures graced many living rooms in the country. The formula for the bittersweet color was created at Smith and no one was able to duplicate it. By far the most famous L.E. Smith pattern is the Moon and Star. It comes in a multitude of designs from jars to cups to canisters and was available in a variety of colors.

In 1975, as the glass industry was waning in the United States, L.E. Smith was purchased by Owens-Illinois. It was sold again in 1986. It closed in 2005, and its equipment and inventory were purchased by William A. Kelman.

The Mount Pleasant Glass Museum

The Mount Pleasant Glass Museum was incorporated in 2013. It honors all three of the glass factories in Mount Pleasant. It is located in the cafeteria of the old Lenox Plant on Route 31. That facility is now called the Mount Pleasant Glass Center.

The exhibit covers 1,800 square feet of space and has some valuable and rare pieces of glass. There is also a small library for research with over one hundred books (and growing). There are three changing exhibits a year, a speaker series and monthly events. It is a growing and valuable contribution to the history of glass.

RYE WHISKEY, RYE WHISKEY

From Wild West towns like Tombstone, Abilene and Cheyenne, to the plush salons of New Orleans, Saint Louis and New York City, rye whiskey was the most popular spirit of eighteenth century America. The thirst for this alcoholic brew traveled as far as the West Indies, France, England, the Philippines and even China. And the best of the rye was Monongahela Rye, manufactured in the Laurel Highlands.

In the late 1700s and early 1800s, the hills and meadows along the Monongahela River were lush with planted rye. The area between modern

Gibsonton Distillery in *History of Westmoreland County. Courtesy of the author.*

Belle Vernon and Monessen was known as the best rye-growing soil in the fledgling nation. It was here, in small cottage industry stills, that the best of the famous Monongahela Rye whiskey was first produced.

In the 1790s, almost every farm in Western Pennsylvania had a still to convert the yearly crop into whiskey. The whiskey was loaded on horses and mules and hauled over the Allegheny Mountains to eastern ports. Then Alexander Hamilton, Secretary of the Treasury, put a tax on whiskey to help pay for the Revolutionary War. A hue and cry arose in Western Pennsylvania that not only tested the new constitution, but brought George Washington back to Pennsylvania at the head of an American army. Although few shots were fired, the confrontation became known as the Whiskey Rebellion (Insurrection). One by one, the whiskey stills began to shut down.

By the 1800s, the manufacture of whiskey became a full-blown industry as dozens of distilleries grew out of the hundreds of dismantled Western Pennsylvania stills. Whiskey was not a year-round production. It usually commenced in October after the harvest and finished sometime in the spring. During that time, thousands of barrels of whiskey were produced and set to age.

Most famous of the regional distilleries were the Sam Thompson Distillery in West Brownsville, the Sam Dillinger Distillery in Ruffsdale, the Abraham Overholt and Company distilleries in both West Overton and Broad Ford and the largest and arguably the best, the John Gibson and Sons Distillery in Gibsonton. Remnants of those world famous distilleries still remain and form the original whiskey trail.

Sam Thompson Distillery

The Sam Thompson Distillery was erected along the National Road in West Brownsville in 1844. There were several massive buildings where the rye was treated and aged into whiskey. Beside one of the red brick buildings was Krepp's Tavern (both still standing), one of the inns along the old National Road, which passed directly in front of it.* It was taken over by the distillery and converted to a gauge and cistern room. The river landing for the tavern was the home of the old Krepp's Ferry, in existence before any bridges were built over the Monongahela. The aged kegs of Sam Thompson were rolled through shoots down the banks of the river to the former ferry landing and onto awaiting keelboats to be transported down the Monongahela to destinations around the country and the world. When Prohibition hit, the product continued to be sold for medicinal purposes. The distillery was sold to Schenley, which still produces Sam Thompson, but not in West Brownsville. Across the river in Bridgeport, now part of Brownsville, the elegant Thompson mansion still stands. It has been restored. It is now a restaurant.

Sam Dillinger Distillery

The Sam Dillinger Distillery, also called the Ruffsdale Distillery, was erected along Glades Path (Route 31) in 1837. It was the second largest distillery in the region. Dillinger was an interesting man who also drove a Conestoga and six-horse team over the National Road, hauling goods from Baltimore. He also had a farm and created some of the first coke ovens and coal mines in the region. His first distillery was in the small

* Krepp was an aide-de-camp to General George Washington during the Revolutionary War.

community of Bethany. It operated for about thirty years before it caught fire and burned to the ground in 1881. So, Sam started all over again, this time in nearby Ruffsdale. His distillery became known as S. Dillinger and Sons. It could produce fifty barrels of whiskey a day, which were stored in barrels in six warehouses. In the 1950s, the Dillinger distillery was sold to Seagrams. They did not use it to make whiskey but used it as a warehouse. It did not close until the 1960s.

Overholt Distillery

There are two Overholt distilleries: one in West Overton and a second at Broad Ford. West Overton was the homestead of the Overholt family. The current distillery building, built in 1859 by Abraham Overholt, grandfather of Henry Clay Frick, is a five-and-one-half story, redbrick and gabled-roof structure now used as a museum. It replaced a former stone distillery, which had replaced a former log distillery. At West Overton, the Overholt brothers produced Old Farm Pure Rye at a capacity of over three hundred gallons a day.

Once Abraham bought out his brothers and partnered with his two sons, a second distillery was built. The distillery at West Overton closed in 1920 because of Prohibition. A number of other buildings remain at West Overton, including the redbrick Overholt home. The entire settlement is on the National Register of Historic Places.

Sitting alongside the Youghiogheny River at Broad Ford is the A. Overholt and Company Distillery. Here the family made Old Overholt Rye. In 1933, the distillery was sold to the National Distillers Products Corporation, which had been selling Old Overholt during Prohibition for medicinal purposes. They moved the production to Cincinnati, Ohio. The massive and strategically placed Broad Ford distillery has been decaying for decades along the shores of the Youghiogheny. Today, new hope for this distillery and the region is emerging with the formation of an energetic group attempting to salvage and restore the distillery, align it with the Coal and Coke Trail and link both to the colonial Braddock's Trail and the modern Great Allegheny Passage. That means jobs, tourists and heritage.

Gibsonton Distillery

The biggest distillery in the United States at the turn of the nineteenth century was the Gibsonton Distillery along the Monongahela River, to the north of Belle Vernon.

John Gibson, an Irishman from Belfast, had established a whiskey business in Philadelphia as early as 1837. In 1856, he purchased over forty acres to build a distillery on the east bank of the Monongahela River, just north of the modern Belle Vernon Bridge. He intended to manufacture wheat and malt whiskey, in addition to the better-known Monongahela Rye.

Construction for the new site began immediately. Limestone was hewn out of the nearby Gibson Quarry, and the cornerstone was put in place. Extra care had to be taken to assure the bonded warehouses could withstand the weight of hundreds of barrels of whiskey, that the temperature of each warehouse was maintained at eighty degrees year round and that no artificial light was used. When the contractors were finished, the site contained eight bonded warehouses, a four-story malt house, a distillery, millhouse, drying kiln, saw mill, boiler, two carpenter shops, a cooper shop, a blacksmith shop and an icehouse. Whiskey was flowing by April 1857.

The cooper shop was where the oaken barrels were made. The process was a long one, with each stave of each barrel aged three years before the barrel was assembled. Then the barrels were assembled by hand without the use of any nails. One person could make only three barrels a day. Once the barrel was filled with whiskey, it either went into the bonded warehouses or was shipped to a buyer. Thus, a continuous need for barrels kept the cooper shop busy. At its peak, five thousand railroad carloads of whiskey-filled barrels were shipped yearly from the distillery.

In 1881, a fire destroyed the distillery building and one large warehouse, but they were quickly rebuilt and by 1882, the distillery employed seventy-five people who churned out enough product to claim they were the "largest rye-distillery in the state and probably in the Union." Manufacturing now included French brandies, which were blended at the plant in Philadelphia from whiskey shipped from Gibsonton.

In 1883, John Gibson died. His son Henry C. Gibson formed a company with longtime associates Andrew M. Moore and Joseph F. Sinnott. The distillery was then known as John Gibson's Son and Company. Production continued to grow until they produced 20,000 barrels of whiskey a year, consuming 1,500 bushels of rye each day.

On December 11, 1882, a cold, cold day when the river was frozen solid, an explosion rocked the distillery and the ensuing fire destroyed warehouse number one, the distillery and the malt houses. The buildings were quickly rebuilt and, by October 1883, were open for business again. But on June 2, 1883, a lantern exploded and fire destroyed warehouses two and three. Seven thousand barrels of whiskey were lost.

By 1884, Henry retired. The company name became Moore and Sinnott and eventually Gibson Distilling Company. The mill converted from coal to natural gas in November 1893, and had its own water supply—directly from the river. The number of workmen's houses now counted 150 and 200 men employed at the plant. They manufactured 150 barrels of whiskey a day at a value of $80 a barrel. The company paid an estimated $750,000 in taxes each year, or $2,000 dollars a day.

The community of Gibsonton was thriving. By 1905, a new seven-story, brick, bonded warehouse was being constructed. Then came Prohibition. In 1920, the Eighteenth Amendment was adopted. It killed the distillery business in the United States. The Gibson Distilling Company went bankrupt. On Tuesday, September 8, 1923, a sheriff's sale was held, and when it was over, nothing remained of the distillery except the buildings. The town nearly became a ghost town.

The Pittsburgh Steel Company acquired the property. In 1926, the limestone buildings were dismantled and the blocks were sold at one dollar a load. People from all over the Mon Valley purchased the stone for their own use. Many valley buildings and walls have a bit of the distillery in them. According to Belle Vernon's newspaper the *Enterprise*, "It is said the Trinity Protestant Episcopal Church of Monessen [688 McKee Avenue] will use a large portion of the stone in erecting a building in that city." The newspaper went on to say, "I wonder if these stones, which once housed whiskey, will save as many souls as the contents sent to hell."

A Stew for the Ages

Does anyone still make possum or squirrel stew? It was a staple around here in pioneer days. No meat markets then. No super Walmarts! If you wanted meat, you had to hunt for it. That took you into the woods with your hound and your gun. I guess you could set traps too. Whatever the method, like Davy Crockett or Christopher Gist or our own pioneers at the crossroad of Glades and Nemacolin paths, someone had to hunt so we could have a squirrel, possum or groundhog in every pot.

Finding or killing the critter was just the beginning. Who was going to clean it? How do you take the skin off? There had to be a system. Was the skin usable, you know, like a buffalo robe to keep you warm? We have all seen a coonskin hat (ah raccoon, another eatable critter), but how about squirrel gloves? And who cured the skins? And how?

If you were lucky enough to find a young animal, you had choices because the meat would be tender. But like a chicken, an old bird is only good for stewing. Well, who cooked it and what did they cook it with? The Internet is loaded with good recipes and good stories about eating game. There was even a cookbook a few years ago by a man from West Virginia called *Road Kill Cookbook*.

After cleaning and cutting, you place the pieces in an iron kettle with a little oil, some garlic, a few onions, some potatoes, tomatoes—wait a minute. Where were you going to get those things too? Our grandparents many times removed could not go to the local grocery store to buy their goodies. They had to "squirrel them away" for when they needed them. Oil could be the grease left over from the last pot of stew you made. Garlic? Forget it. Tomatoes? Not available in America at the time. Onions and potatoes? Well, if you did not plan ahead, you would not have any. If you did not keep some of them to replant the next season, you would not have any more for a long time. How about seasonings: salt, pepper, rosemary, oregano or sage? Here, too, a trip to the woods or a small herb garden had to be maintained. Someone had to tend to it. And where did you find salt? Follow the animals to a saltlick I suppose. They needed salt too. Or, befriend a Native American. They knew where things were in their world. Even the water had to be found and carted into the home.

In these hard times, a trip to the woods might not be a bad idea. There's game everywhere. There are fish waiting in the streams. (Remember there are hunting and fishing rules in our world—something our ancestors did not have to worry about.)

Anyone offering classes on how to make a garden? Or how to find herbs in the woods? Or killing or skinning a critter? Or cooking wild game? Maybe someone should set up a booth during one of the many festivals in the Laurel Highlands featuring a nice wild game stew to see if it is worth the trouble.

JACOBS CREEK

The Monongahela River is only 128 miles long. Jacobs Creek, which is a tributary of a tributary of the Monongahela, is 91 miles long. Can you imagine? The not-so-little northwest-flowing creek drains ten tributaries of its own—including Laurel, Barren, Brush, Shupe and Greenlick Runs—and covers over 98 square miles. The creek begins high in the Chestnut Ridge and cascades down the mountain 785 feet to form the border between Fayette and Westmoreland Counties before it joins the Youghiogheny at the tiny former coal patch called Jacobs Creek.

To the people of the region, Jacobs Creek is legendary. It has featured prominently in historical events through the centuries. Folklore maintains that the creek was named after a Delaware chief named Jacob. He and his tribe spent their lives fishing, trapping and hunting around, in and on its shores. They built paths through its forests of oak, hickory, maple, birch, beech and, of course, chestnut and grew crops in its meadows. Jacob's family

Alliance Furnace, one of the first iron furnaces in the Laurel Highlands. *Courtesy of the author.*

moved on when the Europeans arrived, but Jacob remained behind, fighting to keep his way of life. He lost.

A young George Washington came poking about in 1753 and returned with the English general Edwin Braddock in 1755. They and their men all forded this creek on the way to the founding of the nation. Once the Treaty of Fort Stanwix was signed in 1768, the area around Jacobs Creek opened to settlers. In they came, all kinds, including a Mennonite community that settled at a place they called Pennsville.

One of the first industries along the shores of Jacobs Creek was the mining of salt. Yes, salt. We do not think much about it today, but salt traded equally with gold for many centuries. According to the wonderful little book *Ramblings in the Valley of Jacob's Creek*, published in 1932, settlers were desperate for salt. They would trade a cow or a calf or twenty bushels of wheat for one bushel of salt.

Another early industry at Jacobs Creek was iron. The very first iron furnace west of the Alleghenies, the Alliance Furnace, was built along the creek's southern shores in 1789. It produced many kettles and pots for the pioneers and cannon shot and shells for Mad Anthony Wayne's campaigns against the Indians. The furnace closed in 1802 and was given a Pennsylvania marker in 1946.

A man named James Finley built the first rigid suspension bridge in the United States across the creek's belly in 1801. There is no town there, but there is a bridge. It was an important step in the development of bridges in the world and only cost $600. The bridge was held with chain, and in later years, Finley changed the chain, which was not strong enough, to iron links. A wooden bridge replaced the Jacobs Creek chain bridge in 1833. That, too, is an important type of bridge. One would think a Pennsylvania Marker should identify Finley's bridges.

Of course there was farming. That is the first industry any new settlement must have. There was even an attempt to find oil. When the oil bonanza hit the area around mid-nineteenth century, five wells were dug along Jacobs Creek. They didn't find oil, but they found more salt.

During the era of coal and coke, Jacobs Creek became polluted. But today, it is a happy creek once more as it bubbles and gurgles and makes its way down the mountain to the river.

CROSSIN' THE MOUNTAIN

Most early travelers from New England who wanted to travel west passed through Pennsylvania. The western part of the state, with row after row of hills and ridges from the Appalachian and Allegheny mountain chains, was difficult. Yet the mountains had to be crossed.

In 1810, young Margaret Van Horn wrote about her journey to Ohio with her family. Her diary is currently part of the Gutenberg e-book library under the title *A Journey to Ohio in 1810, as Recorded in the Journal of Margret Van Horn Dwight* and is a fascinating account of the struggle the pioneers endured on their journey west. By the time the family reached the mountains, it was winter, and young Peggy wrote:

> *We set out on foot to reach the height of the mtn—It rain'd fast for a long time, & at length began snowing—We found the roads bad past description,—worse than you can possibly imagine—Large stones & deep mud holes every step of the way—We were oblig'd to walk as much as we possibly could, as the horses could scarcely stir the waggon the mud was so deep & the stones so large—It has grown so cold that I fear we shall all perish tomorrow—We suffer'd with cold excessively, to day…I'm thinking as they say here, we shall be oblig'd to winter on it, for I reckon we shall be unable to proceed on our journey, on account of roads, weather, &c—We are on the old Pennsylvania road—the Glade road is said to be ten times worse than this. That is utterly impossible.*

Peggy and her family would have done well to take the advice of another traveler, William Amphlett. He actually wrote a guidebook for pioneers attempting to cross over the Pennsylvania mountains. He advised:

> *Families proceeding from Philadelphia to Pittsburg to travel in the stage, and to send their goods by the common waggon,* [sic] *taking from the carrier a certificate of their delivery…for in the winter the snows make them impassable for one-horse-carriages; and in the summer the heats are so oppressive that it is dangerous to attempt much, and the emigrant, in the most desirable weather, will be nearly three weeks in accomplishing the journey, if he have any considerable weight of luggage.*

One wonders, if you had to pick up and move your family and your belongings up over the mountain in an old wagon drawn by a few animals, what would you take with you? Space would be limited and there had to be room for fodder for the animals. Electronics are out. What is so important to you that it would take up precious space? That's a good discussion to have over a family dinner.

Another question: What road did Peggy's family take? The Pennsylvania Road? What was that? Where did it start and where did it end? Was it the old Raystown Path? Or the Frankstown Path? We should know Glades Road. It is portions of Route 31 and still passes through the heart of Mount Pleasant.

FISHING THE YOUGHIOGHENY IN THE 1800S

While looking for information about Galley Run—the stream that meets the Youghiogheny River near Broad Ford, just above Connellsville—I recently discovered a wonderful book published in 1904 titled *The History of the Galley Family*.

In addition to information about the family itself, there are wonderful stories on life as it was during the early twentieth century, including one on an unorthodox method people used to catch fish in the Youghiogheny.

Anglers would travel to a stretch of shoreline along the Youghiogheny where pike, suckers or perch were known to congregate. Suckers were always in abundance in the spring after corn planting. Fishermen would find suckers where the stream was shallow and flowed fast. Perch liked still water where they built nests to hold their spawn. The perch season followed the sucker season and lasted about a month. I wonder how many people know these pearls of wisdom today?

To fish with a gun, anglers would find fish, aim and shoot. Fishing in such a manner required use of a long rifle, not our modern-day weapons. They did not aim directly at the fish but below it. On discharge of the weapon, the targeted fish normally would die of percussion shock, roll over and float to the top.

An even more unorthodox method of fishing during that time involved hunting fish with a pitchfork. The activity, known as *gigging*, occurred with anglers employing a three-pronged, steel-tipped fork on a long pole. Gigging was mostly done at night and from a boat. The *giggsman*, as he was called, would travel to a spot known for fish, shine a light, or wooden sticks bundled into a torch, into the water and throw the fork to kill the fish. One nineteenth-century man was known to have caught sixty-two pounds of fish in a single night's gigging session.

A third method of fishing during that time involved using a mat. Called *swabbing*, family and friends would weave a large mat, pack it in a picnic basket and take it to the river. The mat was used to help build a rock dam and enclose fish trapped in the still water.

Such methods of fishing eventually decreased in popularity over the years, but remain no less fascinating.

THE HUNGARIAN WOMEN OF MOREWOOD

It is no surprise to the people of the Connellsville Coke Region that immigrants were hired as labor in the hundreds of coal mines and coke works, big and small, in the area. In the beginning, English, Welsh, Scots and German men worked at the various tasks. When Morewood Mine was opened in 1879, one thousand men—African Americans (a few), Italians (more) and Slavs (the most)—manned the 470 coke ovens. Today we make a distinction between the people of the various Slavic countries, but Poles and Hungarians were also called Slavs when they first came to America.

In 1882, historian George Dallas Albert told an interesting tale about the Hungarian women at Morewood in his book *History of the County of Westmoreland*.[16] It seems that while the men were working at their mining

Morewood Mine. *Courtesy of the author.*

tasks, the women joined them. "Broadbacked and brawny," the women did what they could to ease the burden and fatten the paycheck. These women, Albert stated, "handled the long, heavy iron scraper at the hot mouth of the oven and their burly, dumpy figures are seen between the handles of the big wheelbarrows as they trot from the oven to the car with five or six bushels of coke, weighing from two hundred to two hundred and forty pounds."

What did the bosses at Morewood have to say about the women in the work place? They didn't like it. They did their best to keep them out. They failed. Every time they were chased out of the coke yard, they scurried back in again. Finally management gave up. Their names were not written in the company books. Their labor was not identified. They did not stand in line on payday. They did not get paid. Their husbands did. All the hours of a woman were calculated into her husband's paycheck.

Albert continues to describe these amazing women: "short, almost squat in stature, but broad and strongly built...They all wear boots; that is, for a few months in the winter. In the summer they go barefoot, and even this early are found the strong imprint of plenty of pink toes in the yellow mud. Their skirts are scant, and leave room for about two feet of sunburn below. A distinctive feature of their costume is their head-dress, which usually consists of a shawl, not wrapped turban fashion, but pinned under the chin." We call that a *babushka* (Russian for *grandma* but used to identify this headscarf in America). From medieval times onward, no self-respecting woman would venture outdoors without covering her head. This was true all over Europe and the Middle East.

If you are a coke-region Hungarian, those astounding ladies were your grandmothers. So, if you have any of the garments worn by these courageous women, take them out of the trunk, get them cleaned, put them in a special place in your home (frame them if you can) and treasure them. They are badges of honor.

A HALUPKI IS NOT *ALWAYS* A HALUPKI AND THERE IS NO SUCH THING AS *ITALIAN* TOMATO SAUCE

Food binds everything together. For every holiday, for every picnic, for every special event, both at home and at church, there is food. In the Laurel Highlands, we are blessed because we have food from around the world prepared for us by the expert cooks who brought grandma's recipe from the "old country."

Trouble is, recipes change. There are dozens of reasons why. For example, special ingredients could not be found in America. When that happened, substitutes had to be found: cottage cheese for ricotta, barley for rice or black pepper for red pepper. Sometimes the ingredient was simply eliminated if it could not be found.

Another reason is that someone in your family did not or did like it. Some folks have added garlic to cabbage rolls. Not a true ingredient. In almost every Slavic or Italian region, lamb should be on the menu for Easter. Doubt that is true today—"it's too expensive" and "don't like it" are two major reasons.

Worst of all, a cook will refuse to hand down one key ingredient to the mix, and the taste is not the same. Or they will fail to instruct on how to handle a particular step in the recipe and the taste will change. (Shame on them, for if the recipe is a family heirloom, they have destroyed centuries of tradition.)

On the table at every Eastern European American family's holiday should be a stuffed cabbage dish. But is it a *halupki*, a *sarma*, a *golabki*, or a *mashi*? Which one do you eat? Are you sure it represents your family's heritage or did your mother get the recipe from the neighbor who is not of your heritage at all or did someone in your family change the recipe? Even the name is open to discussion.

The name *halupki* is Slavic, mostly from Yugoslavia. The dish is made with cabbage, rice, pork and sauerkraut, maybe. If you are from Croatia, you should not be eating your stuffed cabbage that way. No, you should call your dish *sarma* and put zero rice in it. That's right. No rice in your cabbage roll and your pork should be smoked too. Maybe that is not quite right, too, for in some regions of Croatia, the recipe is different and rice is on the menu.

The Polish call their cabbage rolls *little pigeons* or *golabki*, and although they use pork, rice and cabbage, they sometimes use barley instead of rice. That is traditional, for rice was not always available.

The Hungarians add two ingredients none of the others seem to use: paprika and sour cream, their traditional staples. Of course they use cabbage, but they pickle it (isn't that sauerkraut?) and they use minced pork too. None of the traditional cabbage roll recipes, regardless of their name, seem to have garlic as an ingredient.

Ukrainians have the biggest variety of preparations. Depending on the region or the season, they might not use cabbage at all. It is what is available: spinach leaves, beet leaves, lettuce leaves and even grape leaves are used. They also pickled their cabbage leaves. More sauerkraut. They call their rolls *halubki* and fill them mostly with one item, rice. Yes, just rice. They may occasionally add some meat or a tomato. Note that the Slavs, the Croatians and the Poles do not mention tomatoes at all, not in the traditional dish.

The closer one moves to the east, the more the variety of stuffed vegetables. Greece stuffs grape leaves and calls them *dolma* (from the Turkish). By the time one reaches the Middle East, everything is stuffed: tomatoes (*tamatum*),

A typical spaghetti dish with Tuscan meat sauce. *Author's photo.*

zucchini (*kosa*), peppers (*filfi rumi*), cabbage (*crum*) and eggplant (*bedingann*). The collection is called *mashi*. None have meat, well, maybe lamb. All use rice. There are different spices including mint, dill and coriander. The grape leaf is now called *wana arnab* and it is smothered with lemon juice. The cabbage roll is as small as a finger and dill is the special ingredient.

So, what is on your table? Is it authentic? If not, who changed it? And why?

Tomato Sauce, You Say?

Things are about the same on the Italian shores too. Julius Caesar and his men ate a form of pasta, but they knew nothing of the tomato. It was brought to Italy from South America after Columbus discovered the continents. That was centuries later. It took the Neapolitans to marry the tomato with pasta (and to put it on flatbread, which we call pizza). Ever since, the variety of tomato sauce is amazing.

Tomato sauce is regional. It is based, like the *halupki*, on what ingredients are available. Two ingredients sure to be in the traditional sauce of the region are tomatoes and garlic. The rest depends on what is grown in or who conquered the region. In the south, Italy is mountainous and barren. No cows but plenty of goats. The south has palm trees and olives. Lots of good oil, no butter. Spices are different too.

In Calabria, one of the key ingredients to tomato sauce is oregano. Oregano came to Calabria with the Greek invasion centuries ago, way before the tomato. So oregano is found in many foods from the south of Italy. There is no meat in a true Calabrian–tomato sauce. Huge chunks of short ribs, sausage and chicken are cooked with the sauce but removed before serving. Once the sauce begins to simmer, meatballs are added.

Abruzzi sauce does not have meat either. It has basil instead of oregano and uses onions. To cut the acidity of the tomatoes, it has a bit of sugar and some baking powder. Neapolitans add parsley and bay leaves to their meatless sauce.

Northern Italians make tomato sauce with meat. They use either ground pork or beef, or both. Northerners add carrots, onions, parsley and garlic to their sauce. Around Bologna, they add a touch of cinnamon. Near Siena, they might add tarragon, which is the signature spice of the town. In Arezzo, they might but more likely will not, add fennel, which is their herb of choice.

Here is a traditional northern tomato sauce, straight from the kitchens of my ancestral village of Quarata near Arezzo in Tuscany:

TUSCAN MEAT SAUCE

4 medium onions
2 cloves garlic
1 ¼-inch-thick slice pancetta
1 large carrot
4 celery ribs
2–3 sprigs fresh parsley
½ cup corn oil
½ tablespoon pepper
½ tablespoon salt
1 pound ground chuck
½ pound pork sausage
4 ounces red table wine (optional)
10 ounces tomato paste
32 ounces whole or crushed
   canned tomatoes
½ cup broth (chicken or vegetable)

Peel onions, wash and cut into quarter wedges. Peel garlic and chop into thirds. Cut pancetta into ½-inch pieces. Peel carrots and celery, wash and cut into 2-inch pieces. Wash parsley. Combine all and grind in a meat grinder or food processor into fine pieces (the grinder is better because it releases the juices).

Place a large iron skillet over medium–high heat. Heat to hot. Add oil. When oil is hot, add all chopped ingredients, pepper and salt; sauté until onions are transparent, stirring often, about 30 minutes. *The longer you cook this mixture, the better your sauce will taste. It is done when it is dark and begins to stick to the skillet.*

When well cooked, add ground chuck and sausage a little at a time, shredding the meat with a fork to form small pieces. Allow to brown until meat is dark brown, about 30 minutes, stirring often so it does not stick. Add one glass of red table wine and continue to sauté. Simmer for 10 minutes on medium-high heat.

When meat is done, add tomato paste to meat mixture, blending well, and let simmer for an additional 15 minutes. When you add the tomato paste to the meat, place crushed tomatoes in puree in a 6-quart pot over low heat and allow to warm. Rinse both tomato and paste cans with broth or water and add to simmering tomatoes.

Remove meat mixture from skillet and add to the simmering tomatoes in 6-quart pot. Put heat on medium-high. When boiling, reduce the heat; allow to simmer slowly for 3 to 4 hours. Stir often to avoid sticking. A good sauce will look dark, almost brown and not red. It is done when oil rises to the top. Skim off excess oil.

YIELD: 2 QUARTS.

Into Fayette County

Broadford: Where It All Began

The great coal and coke empire of Henry Clay Frick began at Broad Ford on his grandfather Abraham Overholt's property. The land was strategic. It sat on the east bank of the north-flowing Youghiogheny River, at a location known by the Native Americans for being a wide (broad) crossing (ford) of the river.

Four men, two of them grandsons of Abraham Overholt, developed a small stretch of land into a coal and coke industry. In less than 2.5 miles, they built over seven coal mines and a railroad (Mount Pleasant & Broad Ford Railroad). These men were the two grandsons, A.O. Tinstman and Henry Clay Frick, and their two partners, Joseph Rist and Colonel A.S.M. Morgan.

In 1817, the same year the railroad opened, Frick founded Frick & Company with Tinstman, who had bought out Rist, and they bought an additional three hundred acres of coal lands surrounding Broad Ford. Frick immediately built 51 coke ovens for his Henry Clay Mine and, within a year, added 150 more for his Frick Mine. By 1889, the original beehive ovens were torn down, and 120 new block beehive coke ovens were built. There were additional ovens for the various mines all the way north to Owensdale and on to Everson, over four miles away.

In 1873, there was a financial crisis in the United States. Tinstman, Risk and Morgan wanted out of Frick and Company. Frick, then only in his twenties, turned to another of his grandfather's friends, Judge Mellon, to borrow $10,000. Mellon,

An aerial view of Morgan Valley with distillery and coal mines. *Courtesy of Larry Hodges.*

ever wary, sent J.B. Corey to see what was happening at Broad Ford. He found Frick living in a cokeburner's cabin. Frick got his money, bought out his partners and was faced with a mortgage that he could not pay. He solved that problem by printing his own money, in the form of script, with which to pay his miners.[17] This idea, born out of necessity by Frick, dominated the coal and coke industry for the next seventy-five years.

By 1882, Frick's holdings had grown considerably. He took on two new partners and reorganized his company into the H.C. Frick Coke Company. By this time, he owned three thousand acres of coal and 1,036 ovens.[18] By 1910, Frick had built twelve mines, but he controlled seventy-eight coke works. He had found his genius.[19]

The Coal and Coke Industry at Broad Ford[◊]

1. RAILROAD BRIDGE

Today, only the cement pillars remain of this once-famous and infamous railroad bridge across the Youghiogheny. It was originally built to connect

---

[◊] Broad Ford is shown two ways: Broad Ford and Broadford. Each is correct based on whether it is a road, a railroad or a place.

the Mount Pleasant and Broad Ford Railroad to the other side of the river. Morris Ramsay, an engineer who would remain with Frick for his lifetime, designed it. According to *The Town that Grew at the Crossroads*, in the 1800s, the Pennsylvania Railroad and the B&O Railroad were fighting for dominance in the coalfields. Somehow the Pennsylvania got the B&O to move their rolling stock south across the river. Then, the good men at the Pennsylvania set that bridge on fire so the B&O could not come back.[20] If the timeline is correct, that is when Frick sold his railroad and its bridge to the B&O.

2. COKE OVENS
The coke ovens erected in this area were the first for Frick. There were two main batteries of block beehive ovens. Those along the lower right, parallel to the river and in front of the distillery, were originally constructed by Frick for the Henry Clay Mine. The second battery ran north to south along what is now called the Broad Ford Road and served the Frick Mine. Additional ovens ran along the railway up and beyond Owensdale, along the route of Galley Run. Until a few decades ago, the remnants of these ovens remained.

3. HENRY CLAY WORKS
The Henry Clay Mine was one of the few mines actually built by Frick. In fact, it was his first mine and opened in 1871. The entire complex was designed and built by Morris Ramsay, who, by 1884, was the Mining Engineer for all of Frick's holdings. The mine entrance was a slope entrance, meaning the seam of coal was near enough to the surface that the men could walk into the mine and gently go downhill to the seam. By 1888, the general superintendent was Thomas Lynch, another man who would stay with Frick and run his coal and coke empire from the offices at Scottdale. The mine operated for about twenty years before it was closed in the early 1890s. The entrance, however, continued to be used to enter the Rist Mine that was less than half a mile to the north.

3A. COMPANY STORE
Located to the south of the main road, within the distillery complex, was the first known Frick "company store." Company stores were necessary because mines were erected in rural areas. When Frick bought out his partners, during the Panic of 1873, he had cash flow problems. Cleverly, Frick invented company script, to be used by his miners at what would soon be called the Union Supply Company. The invention of script saved Frick and became an industry-wide standard throughout the coal industry. He was able to use hard-to-come-by United States currency to meet his loans. By the 1950s,

Frick had 116 Union Supply Company stores and was able to undercut the entire market because he could order in huge quantities. Contrary to the legends that exist today, Frick's prices were always competitive with the local market. That was not true of some of the other operators. The building is gone today.

4. BROADFORD HOTEL
With a distillery and a bevy of coal mines, Broad Ford began to thrive. Soon a hotel was needed to service all the people who came to sell equipment and observe the various industries in the Morgan Valley. Owned and operated by Julius Schlinger, the hotel remained in operation well into the 1960s, far beyond the heyday of coal and coke. Today, even the foundation is gone.

5. FRICK MINE
The Frick Mine was near to the Henry Clay. It stood to the west of the road and the rail lines. It was built in 1871, had a drift entrance and, like most of the mines in this area, did not have a large enough seam to last more than twenty years. It was incorporated into the Rist Mine in 1882 and was exhausted by 1889. As for the additional names, it appears there was never a Broadford Mine. Probably, the Frick was sometimes called the Broadford. Likewise, the name Novelty never seems to appear in the same list where the Frick is listed. Some say this was Frick's first mine. More research is needed.

6. RIST MINE
The Rist Mine was the last of the Morgan Valley mines to be built. In fact, it consolidated a number of mines in the valley. In 1882, the Eagle, Foundry, Frick and Morgan mines, along with their long string of bank coke ovens, were combined into one large, more efficient mine: Rist. The slope entrance to the Rist Mine was less than half a mile from the Henry Clay. Its entrance was just to the right of the modern road. Little can be seen today, but there was a full facility here, including a tipple (built by Morris Ramsay), coal bins, an engine house, a seven- and one-half-foot round ventilating shaft and tipple house. The entrance collapsed many years ago. In 1885, 41 miners and 3 boys were working at the mine and 11 persons were in the offices.[21] In 1915, there were 101 persons employed at this mine.[22]

7. MORGAN MINE
Built in 1869 by Tinstman and Morgan, under the company name of Morgan and Company, Frick acquired the Morgan Mine in 1872 when he

merged his holdings with Morgan and Tinstman. It had a slope entrance to the left or western side of the Broadford Road and was situated about fifty feet behind the coke ovens. It was less than one-quarter mile from the Henry Clay Mine, and a nearby stop on the Mount Pleasant and Broadford Railway was (and is) called Morgan Station. In fact, an article in the *Connellsville Weekly Courier* in 1918 calls the entire area Morgan Valley. That same article lists the abandoned Frick mines for sale in Morgan Valley to include Valley, Morgan, Rist, Tip Top, Foundry, White, Novelty and Summit (note: no Frick or Henry Clay).[23]

8. FOUNDRY MINE (SUMMIT NO. 3)

Built in 1870 by Strickler and Lane, Foundry Mine's stop along the railway was at Sherrick Station. In 1889, eighty of the hundreds of bank coke ovens that lined Galley Run belonged to Foundry. By 1906, there were ninety-seven. It was sold to Frick in 1879. Foundry had a drift entrance to the west of the Broadford Road and was connected to Eagle Mine underground. The 1882–83 report from the Pennsylvania mining inspectors did not give it a good rating, claiming that it "in general is in a bad condition," and many of its miners were working "beyond the air."[24] Mines had big fans for ventilation. Sometimes the fans were not big enough to deliver air deep into the mine or "beyond the air." It merged with Risk in 1882, was closed in 1888 and abandoned in 1918. As with many abandoned mines, Foundry caught fire in the mid-twentieth century and burned well through the 1950s. After the fire was extinguished, locals would go to the mine to gather "red dog" (the remains of burned coal) to use for roads.

9. WHITE MINE (GLOBE)

Built in 1873 by Charles Armstrong, the White Mine was purchased by A.A. Hutchinson and Brothers before being acquired by Frick in 1877. According to the *Keystone Courier*, after Frick purchased this mine, he owned the entire four and one-half mile string of coke ovens from Broad Ford to Everson.[25] White was a drift mine, and by 1906, it had two hundred coke ovens. In 1881, the great immigration of central and southern Europeans began in the Connellsville Coke Field. The second group of central Europeans to arrive in the United States to work in the Connellsville Coke Fields was 40 men who were sent to work in the Morgan Valley at the Eagle and White mines.[26] By 1915, 107 men were employed, many of them Slovak, Italian, Hungarian and Polish.[27] They had pushed out the Welsh, Scots and Germans who worked the mines before them. The White Mine was closed in 1919.

10. EAGLE MINE (SUMMIT NO. 1 AND SUMMIT NO. 2)

Built 1868 (some say 1870) by Sherrick, Markle and Company, the Eagle had a drift opening and eighty beehive coke ovens. It was acquired by Frick in 1880 and was combined with Rist in 1882. There were two pit entries to this mine, and some reports say they became Summit No. 1and Summit No. 2. By 1900, Eagle was worked out. It closed in 1917. The relationship between Eagle and Summit is not clear at this time. It appears that James Cochran (Cochran and Kiester) began a Summit Mine in 1874, before Eagle was built. In the *Connellsville Courier*, a weekly column called *Report of the Operation and Output of the Coke Ovens of the Connellsville Region*, which ran for years, Eagle and Summit are listed as two separate mines operating at the same time.

In 1918, the H.C. Frick Coke Company, in order to divest itself of unwanted property, put the abandoned mines of Morgan Valley up for bid. The eight plants included: Morgan, Rist, Tip Top, Foundry, White, Novelty (supposedly the Frick) and Summit. Most of the mines were expected to sell for between $15,000 and $40,000.[28] One of the reasons Frick divested himself of the Morgan Valley mines was the development of the byproduct coke oven. When coal was being turned into coke, there were many byproducts that could be sold to other industries for profit. In the beehive ovens, these products were lost, simply dispersing into the air. With the new ovens, the various gases could be trapped and saved. A second reason these mines became less appealing is that the industry was turning to the rivers for shipments, leaving the railroads out of the picture. Finally, and most important of all, the Pittsburgh seam, often nine to fifteen feet high, which ran, and still runs, underground in the Connellsville area, simply was mined out in this region.

ADELAIDE MINE: A LONG HISTORY

One of the oldest mines in the Connellsville Coal Field was the Adelaide Mine along the Youghiogheny River in Fayette County. Unlike many mines in the region, the Adelaide had longevity, not closing until well into the 1940s.

The Adelaide Mine was originally called Cupola and was constructed in or near a town called Maysville.[29] Opened for operation in 1888, the

Cupola Mine had a shaft opening and was located on the southern side of the Youghiogheny River, along the McKeesport and Youghiogheny Rail Road. The H.C. Frick Coke Company purchased the small facility in 1889 and rebuilt it. It is one of the few mines that Frick actually constructed. Mostly, he purchased mines.

Once Frick purchased the mine, the name was changed to Adelaide. The reason for the change was that there was another Cupola Station located on the Pennsylvania Rail Road in central Pennsylvania, near Harrisburg, and shipments of material needed at Frick's Cupola Mine had been erroneously delivered to the wrong location.[30] There is controversy as to just which Adelaide had the mine named in her honor. Today, sources maintain that the mine was named for Henry Clay Frick's wife, who was called Adelaide. This is not unusual, as many of the mines in our region were named after family members. However, several newspaper articles tell a different story. In 1953, the *Connellsville Daily Courier* reported, "But I do know how it was called Adelaide. It was when James Asa Childs married Miss Adelaide Hogg. The late Henry Clay Frick was a brother-in-law of James Childs and he named it after Adelaide Hogg. James Childs always used to be kidded about the peculiar name of his wife. But he was so well liked that the Adelaide employees bought him a beautiful red horse for his wedding present. And in turn Mrs. Childs gave a big party for the whole town."[31] The oral history of the newspapers is wrong. Childs was the brother-in-law of Henry Clay Frick because Frick married Childs's sister Adelaide. Childs, who was superintendent at Adelaide from 1895 to 1906, did marry a Hogg. Her name was Mary Belle Hogg. Adelaide Mine was named after Henry Clay Frick's wife, Adelaide.[32]

The layout of Adelaide followed a pattern that would be repeated throughout the district. The coke ovens were constructed in a linear pattern, along the southern side of the railway, in order for the coke to be easily conveyed to the awaiting rail cars. The entrance to the mine was located to the south of the coke ovens, high on the hillside. The tipple and its structures cascaded down the hillside in order to transport the newly mined coal to the coke ovens. Frick also constructed houses: 125 houses were originally built (by 1959, only 34 remained); some of them were duplexes to accommodate more than one mining family. Located to the north of the railway and next to the river, the houses were built in a linear manner too. The layout of all of the "patches" was ultimately determined by the layout of the land.

Miners outside of the Adelaide Mine. *Courtesy of the author*.

The Battles of 1891

In 1891, the Connellsville Coke Region was in turmoil over wages, hours and conditions. In April, ten families were evicted from Morewood, in Westmoreland County. Then a massacre occurred at Adelaide, in Fayette County. The workers at Adelaide were mainly Hungarian and Irish. Language was a barrier, for many of the workers could not speak English and were unsure exactly what was happening and why. In addition to the local sheriff, Company C was called to deal with the striking miners. By May 8, seven thousand "Negros and Italians" were expected to reach the coalfields to replace the miners.[33] Evictions continued at "Adelaide, Sterling, Broad Ford, Leisenring No. 3, Morewood and Standard. The evicted families are tenting out and living wherever they can. Fifteen families at Broad Ford are quartered in a hall. Many of the homeless are taken in and cared for by comrades."[34] Eventually things settled down. The miners won few concessions.

Frick's Largess

After the 1891 horror in the coalfields, Frick tried to keep his men from striking. He did that by anticipating demands and providing them before they were demanded. He began safety programs that made his mines the safest in the industry. He provided his workers with the best housing at the cheapest cost to them. His wages were the highest in the industry. He tried to create his own unions. Henry Clay Frick is known for being ruthless. Most of that reputation is due to the events at Homestead in 1892. He may also have been ruthless when it came to competitors, for it wasn't long before the H.C. Frick Coke Company owned most of the mines in the Connellsville district. But when it came to his mines, his miners and his patches, there was a humanity that pushed other mine owners to improve their conditions.

As early as 1889, the Frick company was donating land to erect schools. Adelaide's school began construction that same year.[35] By 1914, Frick miners were receiving pensions. During that year, 612 men were added to the pension lists, bringing the total to 2,704 men on pension. The average age was 63.3, the average years of service 28.6, and the monthly pension was $20.40. At Adelaide, Frick paid $1,494.25 that year.[36] That amount was for approximately 73 Adelaide retirees.

And there was more. In addition to safety programs, Americanization classes and garden competitions, Frick built recreational facilities for his miners and their families. Playgrounds were built in the patches, with swings, sand-boxes and see-saws. There were even swimming pools. Frick created a baseball league and paid for uniforms, equipment, grandstands and maintenance of the fields. He also absorbed the management of schedules and awards. Adelaide's team was managed by Martin Hasson and, after him, Walter Ramsey.[37] There were also bands. Adelaide's band was led by John Fuchrer.

Some say Frick made these improvements in order to keep the growing trend toward unionization away from his mines. It really doesn't matter, for the life of the miner both in and out of the mine was better under Frick than any other operator. Interestingly, the villages were gated communities with guards.

The Rise and Fall of Adelaide

Adelaide Mine continued to develop as an important site. By 1901, it had a slope and an eighty-one-foot-deep shaft, 375 beehive coke ovens and three hundred employees. The fate of Adelaide can be told through the statistics of its coke ovens. These statistics come from the *List of Coke Ovens in the Connellsville District*, which was printed weekly for decades in the *Connellsville Weekly Courier*. It is an excellent source of information about all the mines in the Connellsville District. It provides the name of the owner and tells how many coke ovens were in blast: a barometer of good times and bad. For us, it is a simple way to find out about the owners and the ovens of Adelaide.

At the end of December 1917, the Adelaide Mine had 260 of the original 375 ovens, with 190 in blast and was still owned by the H.C. Frick Coke Company.[38] In 1918, the conditions at Adelaide remained the same. In 1919, only 120 furnaces were in blast, and by 1920, none of the Adelaide coke ovens were in operation. From 1920 to '24, the Adelaide ovens were silent. There were two reasons for this: tough economic conditions in America and the need for major improvements in both coke ovens and mine equipment. The improvements required a major investment. Was there enough coal remaining at Adelaide to make these changes? Frick thought no. In 1925, Adelaide fell from the list entirely. It remained unlisted until 1926, and at that time, some of the changes that were needed seem to have been accomplished, but not by Frick.

The firm of Corrado Coal and Coke, Incorporated purchased the Adelaide Mine. There might have been another owner before Corrado: the Abraham Coal Mining Company. *The Fourth Industrial Directory of the Commonwealth of Pennsylvania* lists the Abraham Coal Mining Company and the Pittsburgh Wood Preserving Company as the only industries in Adelaide in 1922.[39] Little is known about the Abraham Coal Mining Company, but it was listed as a new coal company in the *Weekly Courier* in 1917 when Frick still owned the Adelaide Mine.[40] John Aubrey Enman, who wrote one of the definitive books on the Connellsville Coke District, distinctly states that the H.C. Frick Coke Company closed the Adelaide Mine in 1923.[41] That same year, the Abraham Coal Mining Company was up for sheriff's sale.[42] Also in 1923, the Adelaide Coal Company, owned by G. Corrado, dissolved.[43] Yet in 1929, the *Daily News Standard* of Uniontown reported that "orders are continuing to pour in for coal mined at Adelaide and the demand has caused an additional force of men to be added.[44] This was followed by an ad in the *Daily Courier* in July of the same year calling for coal miners to apply to the superintendent at Adelaide mine of the Corrado and Gailardi Incorporation.[45] So, the Adelaide mine was experiencing a number of owners and was doing poorly. Most of the industrial coal from this mine was gone, and it was moving toward subsistence mining: small quantities for homes and small businesses.

Beehive, Battery, Furnace and Merchant Ovens

While the Corrado company was struggling to survive in the competitive coal business, it must have decided new and different ovens would bring better opportunities. Corrado removed many of the old beehive battery ovens at Adelaide and erected one hundred merchant ovens, all of them in blast in 1926. By December of the same year, none of the merchant ovens were in blast. This continued through 1930, and by 1931, there were only forty ovens at Adelaide, with all forty in blast. These forty ovens were newly built, so many, if not all, of the furnace coke ovens were torn down or abandoned.[46]

The circular beehive oven was the oven used in the Connellsville Coke Fields for years. Eventually the beehive ovens were built side by side along railroad tracks and joined together by an additional rectangular structure, linking them in a long straight line that was easily loaded onto railroad cars. Frick sold his coke to steel mills which needed furnace

Building beehive coke ovens at Standard Shaft mine near Mount Pleasant. *Courtesy of Jim Lozier.*

coke for their blast furnaces. Corrado did not have such contracts and probably did not expect to get any. So, Corrado made a major investment to build merchant ovens, also known as by-product ovens. When ovens were first built in the coalfields the primary purpose was to turn coal into coke. Ultimately someone thought of a way to capture all the gases that were simply dissipating into the air and sell them as a secondary industry. These byproducts included hydrogen, methane, ethane, carbon monoxide, carbon dioxide and a few more. Finally the entire industry was creating byproduct ovens. Unfortunately for Corrado, by 1934, only seventeen of the forty merchant ovens were in blast.[47]

In 1946, the Adelaide mine was still owned by the Corrado and Gailardi Coal Company and fifty men were working there. That same year, the Adelaide Mine was cited for delinquent taxes for 1940 to 1943.[48]

There were additional owners since the 1940s, none of them working the mine, as it was in its heyday. When the mines closed, the miners purchased some of the houses, but most were demolished. A few still stand. There are definitely no beehive ovens at Adelaide.

Legacy of the Adelaide Mine

Adelaide, as with all the mines in the region, has left us with pollution problems. Water was always an issue in mines: either not enough of it or, more often, too much of it. Each coke oven needed hundreds and hundreds of gallons of water a day to quench the coke. So, every mine was built near a stream—a river, a creek or a smaller tributary. It is also the reason that many of the water companies in the region were created, built and maintained by coal companies. After the water quenched the coke, it flowed back to where it came from, taking with it the filth generated by the burn. As early as the 1920s, the state was struggling with pollution problems from abandoned mines.

Mines had other water problems too. They would flood. If the nearby stream swelled, the mine flooded. If one of the tunnels hit an underground pocket of water, it would flood, too. When the mine flooded, the mine had to be closed, and the men were out of work. Huge pumps had to run constantly to keep the water from flooding the mine. Frick helped solve some of the problem by connecting his mines underground. For example, Adelaide along the Youghiogheny River was linked to the Trotter Mine a few miles to the south. Thus, water flowed freely between the two (so did workers). However, once the mines were closed, the pumps were shut down and the water, polluted by the underground chemicals, flowed through the linking mines and into the streams, causing pollution. "By the time the coal was depleted in early 1961 the last mines operating in the field were pumping 25 million gallons of water a day to the surface. Less than two years after the mines were abandoned and pumping was stopped the mine water discharged north of Uniontown near Phillips appeared, indicating that the pool had filled and was overflowing. Other major discharge points from the south basin have since appeared at Adelaide and Henry Clay mines on the Youghiogheny River."[49]

Eventually the Adelaide Mine entrance was sealed. By sealing the mine, it kept out people who could get into trouble. But—and more importantly—it helped curb pollution. With the pumps gone and the entrance sealed, water would fill the mine and be contained (Water would also put out fires within the mine.).

Today, the town of Adelaide is having a bit of a rebirth. It sits on the Great Allegheny Passage. It has a campground and many visitors. Some of the coke ovens can still be seen along the passage, and the sealed mine entrance remains high on the hill. The smoke and stench of burning coal is gone. What remains is a picturesque scene along the Youghiogheny River.

Brownsville's Historic Districts

Three important factors in the growth of America were its rivers, its roadways and, finally, its railroads. Brownsville, Pennsylvania, profited from all three. Its rich and diverse history and the heroic efforts of its contemporary citizens have kept its historical integrity intact.

Brownsville sits on the edge of a cliff, overlooking the Monongahela River. It is a perfect place for an early colonial town. That's what Colonel James Burd of the Ohio Company thought as he traveled Nemacolin Path from the top of Chestnut Ridge to the river. He built the first fort on the cliff in the 1759. It became known as Redstone Old Fort, in honor of the Native American mounds (that still exist) found there. Explorers called them "old forts."

Burd was followed by Thomas and Basil Brown, who founded Brownsville in 1785. Its location made the tiny community the hub of activity for over two hundred years. As pioneers made their way west over Nemacolin Path and later the National Road, they would stop at Brownsville, make their way down the steep cliff and either cross the river by ferry or sell their wagons and buy boats to head west by river. So, Brownsville became a boat center. The yards built flatboats, keelboats (Lewis and Clark Expedition) and eventually the incredible steamboats that plied the Western waters and opened the nation to exploration and settlement. Orders for shallow-hulled steamboats flowed into the Brownsville and West Brownsville yards—boats destined for the New Orleans trade, boats for the Red River, boats for the furthest reaches of the Missouri and even boats for the Civil War. The yards built side-wheelers, sternwheelers, big boats and small boats. Most hauled goods, including coal for the steel mills, steel for the factories along the watershed, cattle, cotton, lead, iron ore and the newly discovered commodity—Titusville oil.

In the late nineteenth and early twentieth century, Brownsville remained a transportation hub. This time it played an important role in the coke and coal era. That is when the railroad used the community to gather and ship the coal and coke from the greatest coalfield in the United States. They did this through an underground tunnel, but more on that later.

Practically the entire community—fewer than three thousand souls—is historic. There is a lot to see and even more to save. Some parts of Brownsville have been carefully preserved, thanks to thousands of hours of volunteer work and millions of dollars of grants and donations. Other parts of the community are still in various levels of decay, awaiting someone to take on the challenge of restoration and preservation. For well over twenty years,

Nemacolin Castle as seen from the garden. *Author's photo.*

two districts have been designated historic: the North Side Historic District (circa 1785–1943) and the Commercial Historic District (1835–1943). Their legacy centers on transportation and coal.

It is on the cliff that one finds the earliest hidden treasures of Brownsville. Three streets, now known as the North Side Historic District, hold mansions, commercial buildings and churches that bespeak of the history of the nation. It is the oldest commercial/residential district west of the Alleghenies. It encompasses a six-block area, with 186 of 230 structures of historical significance. The alleyways bear such names as Peddlers, Traders and Hatters. A lot of history took place here. The names of the men who populated the district with their families read like a who's who of America.

Three parallel streets dominate: Front (Nemacolin Path and the original business district), Market (the National Road and U. S. 40) and Church (where Brownsville still goes to worship). It is the best-kept secret in southwestern Pennsylvania.

Front Street

Most stunning among the buildings on the north side is the castle: a Tudor-style building, complete with towers, known as Nemacolin Castle (136 Front Street). The original trading post erected by Jacob Bowman sits in its heart. The twenty-two-room interior contains many original furnishings. The grounds have a spectacular view of the Monongahela River and valley. It is on the National Register of Historic Places.

One exits the castle onto tree-lined, majestic Front Street. Front Street was built directly on the Nemacolin Trail. It was the main thoroughfare of the community prior to the coming of the National Road and once ran all the way down the steep cliff to the river. Today, traffic must stop at the castle. It is graced with glorious and well-maintained homes from Greek Revival, Gothic Revival, Queen Anne and Victorian Eclectic styles. They date to the late eighteenth and early nineteenth centuries, and most were first used as commercial/residential enterprises. Today, the area is residential.

The spirits of great men can be found on Front Street. There are riverboat captains: Captain Z.W. Carmack plied his boats along the Monongahela River, Captain Valentine Geisey served in the War of 1812 and was the official host to the Marquis de Lafayette when he visited Brownsville in 1825 and, perhaps the most famous of all, Captain Henry Shreve. Of all the men who navigated the Mississippi watershed, Henry Shreve is second only to Robert Fulton in importance, and he might even be more important than Fulton. Fulton married the steam engine with the boat and sent it from the Monongahela River all the way down the Ohio and Mississippi to New Orleans, thus, enhancing trade. But, as with every boat before him, he could not bring his steamboat back north against the current and dismantled it in New Orleans. Shreve and his partners in Brownsville built a stronger engine and put it in a shallow-hulled boat they called the *Enterprise* and sent it on its way. Once Shreve and his boat reached New Orleans, he turned the boat around and brought it back to Brownsville. That opened the entire watershed to two-way traffic and that opened the entire nation to trade, expansion, and immigration.

Philander C. Knox, a lawyer by profession, was a United States senator from Pennsylvania, Attorney General of the United States under presidents McKinley and Roosevelt and Secretary of State to President Taft. Then he ran for president against Warren G. Harding. He was a Brownsville citizen and lived on Front Street. He may well be Brownsville's most famous citizen. His home (322 Front Street) was originally built in 1816 and occupied by

The Philander Knox House on Front Street in Brownsville. *Courtesy of the author.*

Jacob Goodlander, a clockmaker. The lovingly restored home is on the National Register of Historic Places and a marker stands in front of its stucco façade.

In the middle of the block stands the Brownsville Academy (401 Front Street). It was originally built as an inn but later became a Woman's Seminary. Many young Brownsville girls learned to read and write and do needlework at the academy. It later became a newspaper office where the *Free Lance* was published. The hitching post and coach step still remain at the curb.

Important events also took place on Front Street. Next to the castle is a building that has remnants of the Black Horse Tavern (203 Front Street). Established in the 1780s, it was one of Brownsville's first inns. The tavern was the first and last meeting place of unhappy participants of the Whiskey Rebellion. On July 27, 1791, men from the surrounding area gathered in anger over the colonial government's tax on whiskey. Farmers in the region, eager to get their crops to market, found it cheaper to send whiskey east instead of rye: a mule could carry only four bushels of rye, but twenty-four bushels of rye made into whiskey. Thus, the first test of our Constitution was to be over taxation, the very issue that had led to our successful rebellion against England. The Whiskey Rebellion ended here three years later on August 28, 1794.

Another marvel of Front Street is the Samuel E. Taylor House (209 Front Street). It is not so much what happened here as to the building itself. The ceilings are twelve feet high, the doors are nine feet high, and each room has a fireplace. It was lovingly maintained for many years and is a gem. The interior contains fifteen large rooms, including a ballroom, smoking room, parlor and library. Features include seven fireplaces, mahogany wainscoting, a grand staircase, pocket doors, window seats, stained glass windows and a leaded, beveled glass entryway. The carriage barn behind the house is the last standing stable within borough limits.

Market Street

The National Road bypassed Front Street and created Market Street. Like the Nemacolin Path, the road ran down Market Street all the way to the river and it still does. Upper Market Street became the commercial center of Brownsville. Banks and shops moved from Front Street to Market Street. Upper Market Street is as wide today as it was when the National Road was first built. That is plenty wide. One can almost see the wagons hitched in front of the stores. Most of the existing buildings are the same ones that were built for the National Road.

Not only did the goods of the nation travel on Market Street, so did the amazing and interesting travelers. They would stop at William P. Searight's dry goods store (411 Market Street) to pick up a shirt or get their shoe repaired by Christian P. Gummert (409 Market Street). The stagecoaches stopped at Brashear Tavern (517–523 Market Street), which was there long before the National Road. Basil Brashear built it around 1797, and it remained his tavern until 1846. It is arguably the oldest structure still standing in Brownsville. The building is German farmhouse–style.

Among the travelers who stopped at Brashear were politicians from as far as Kentucky on their way to Washington D.C., including Andrew Jackson and General Lafayette, who visited Friendship Hill in 1825 and paused here and spoke to the citizens from the door of Brashear Tavern.

Brashear Tavern has one more tale to tell: John A. Brashear, astronomer and educator, was born here in 1840. Brashear became the preeminent astronomer and manufacturer of astronomical instruments in the United States.

He built his first telescope in 1875, and nearly all astronomical spectroscopes and spectrographs were made under his supervision, including astrophysical instruments and army and navy rangefinders, gun sights and meridian instruments. The tavern is on the National Register of Historic Places.

Church Street

The third street in the district is Church Street, one street north of Market. Church Street houses a number of nineteenth-century homes (and even the former hospital and nurse's residence), but is known for its religious buildings. The most prominent among them is Saint Peter's Roman Catholic Church (Church and Shaffner Streets). Irish stonemasons built the church of locally quarried, hand-hewn stone in 1845, to replace a former building, in anticipation of Brownsville being named a cathedral city (it was not). It is the oldest continuously operating church in Western Pennsylvania, the first parish in Fayette County. It's one of the finest examples of provincial Gothic architecture in America and was reported in *Ripley's Believe It or Not* to have the only heated grave in the world. It was named to the National Register of Historic Places on October 15, 1980.

Another outstanding church on Church Street is the Christ Episcopal Church (305 Church Street). It was erected in 1859 of cut sandstone. The building is stunning with beautiful stained-glass windows (some from Tiffany), a slate roof and stone buttresses. More importantly, the graveyard in the back of the building contains the graves of Jacob Bowman, who was the postmaster and built Nemacolin Castle; Thomas Brown, the founder of Brownsville; and John H. and Archibald Washington, believed to be cousins of George himself.

When Philander Knox walked from Front Street on a Sunday and John A. Brashear from Market, they came to the First United Methodist Church (215 Church Street). The Methodists had a presence in Brownsville since 1776, when they worshiped in a log cabin on the very spot.

Over the Hill

Today, Market Street appears to cross over the Monongahela River via the high Lane Bane Bridge. It does not. Just before the bridge, there is a turn to the right and under the bridge. That is Market Street following the route

Launching a boat at the boatyard in Brownsville. *Courtesy of the author.*

of the National Road down a section called the Neck to the modern-day downtown of Brownsville.

In addition to boatyards, the Commercial Historic District (1835–1943) in downtown Brownsville also held a bevy of businesses including foundries, banks, a railroad hub and even a coal mine. To cross the river, there was a covered bridge. Near the bottom of Market Street (then and now), is the Flatiron Building (69 Market Street). Its uniqueness is in its shape, round in the front with a peaked roof, looking like an antique flatiron ready for pressing clothes. Only a few similar buildings are known to exist in the United States today. It was restored in the 1990s by the Brownsville Area Revitalization Corporation (BARC) and now houses a museum and visitor's center.

The massive Union Station (59 Market Street), built by the Monongahela Railway Company, overshadows the Flatiron Building. Constructed in 1927, passenger trains left the depot every twenty minutes for destinations around the country.

Between them are a few railroad structures remaining from the heyday of the coal and coke industry: the freight depot, the railroad express office and the coal tunnel. The latter is the most fascinating, for it is an underground tunnel that passes through the coal mines of the region. The mined coal was put aboard the conveyor belt and transported to the river, where it was loaded and freighted

The historic cast iron bridge over Dunlap's Creek in Brownsville. *Courtesy of the author.*

to its destination. There were several belts of this nature in the coal district; this one may be the end of the Palmer Coal Dock serving the Footdale, Buffington, Lambert and Ralph mines. Their coal was carried via underground rail to the Filbert mine where a rotary mine car dumper was awaiting them. At Filbert, the dumper moved the coal onto a conveyor belt that carried it nearly three miles to the Palmer Coal Dock on the shores of the Monongahela River here at Brownsville. The reason for these two-tunnel systems was to eliminate the coke ovens in their various mines and ship the coal to the Monongahela River, which had become cheaper than moving the coal by train.

There are a number of other structures in the once-thriving Brownsville downtown before the National Road crosses the Cast Iron Bridge. Although they need a bit of a cleanup, their façades are outstanding and worth taking the time to walk around and "ohh" and "ahh" at the marvel of it all.

There was no way to get from Brownsville to what was then called Bridgeport, other than to construct a bridge over Dunlap's Creek. The first bridge collapsed under the weight of a horse and carriage, but the current one was built between 1836–39 by the United States Army Corps of Engineers. It is a marvel of engineering. It is the first rib-fixed metal arch bridge erected in the United States and paid for by the United States government. It is a single-span, cast-iron structure with cast iron fabricated in Brownsville. It is eighty feet long and thirty feet wide. More than 150 years later, it is still in use, with very little structural changes. The bridge is a National Historic Civil Engineering Landmark and is listed on the National Register of Historic Places.

Beyond are other treasures too: Fiddles' Confectionary (101 Bridge Street) is a great place to get old-fashioned pancakes, hot dogs, hamburgers and ice cream served in 1950s style booths with the graffiti carvings still intact; the Thompson House, now a restaurant for fine dining; the Brownsville Brewery building, now a dry cleaner; the railroad shops and the small Bridgeport coal patch town, complete with still-standing outhouses (now used for storage); and the Bridgeport coal mine itself, with many of the buildings still standing.

Brownsville is still quite a treasure.

Camp Wesco

When I was five or six years old, I went to a wilderness camp somewhere on Laurel Mountain. I was the youngest little scout to ever set foot in the place, and the counselors were not sure they wanted me to stay. But my mother insisted that if there was any trouble, she would come and get me. That week introduced me to the wonderful world of nature and travel and life beyond the mundane. After that, I went year after year, until I grew out of that wanderlust and into another.

I may have lost the location, but I never forgot the name. That camp was Camp Wesco. When I moved closer to the mountains, I went looking for the camp that played such an important part in my early life. I knew it was near Stahlstown. That's all I knew. But I found it along Route 130. That is, I found the two pillars that were the gates. We could not enter because a cleverly built pile of earth blocked the way.

I wanted more. I wanted to drive up the dirt track to the open meadow where the Adirondack-style cabins (with open sides) lay. There were three cabins for the Peter Pan group (the youngest) and three more for Robin Hood. In that meadow, there was a huge stone and wood dining hall to accommodate

Author and friends at Camp Wesco in the 1950s. *Courtesy of the author.*

all the campers. No paper plates back then. We ate on china. We had real glasses. We ate balanced meals put together by a certified nutritionist.

There were other buildings too. Next door to the huge dining hall were a small infirmary, a third building that my memory cannot conjure and a wonderful crafts cabin. There, we wove lariats out of plastic-coated wire and did other neat things, too. I loved it.

There was a swimming pool, too. It was big and dark green from the chlorine. I earned my swimming badge and my lifeguard certificate there. We went hiking. We sang around the campfire. We roasted marshmallows at the end of long skinny sticks. We were afraid snakes were waiting for us in the outhouses!

Beyond the meadow and down hand-hewn stairs with tree branch railings were two more groups of cabins: Pirates and Pioneers. Up in the hills were the Gypsies. They did not have cabins. They lived in tents and cooked over an open fire. We were in awe of them whenever they came down to the dining room to eat, which wasn't often.

Imagine my surprise when I began to research Camp Wesco and discovered that it was founded around 1924 (way way before my time). Camp Wesco began as a boy's camp, but it wasn't long before the girls got two weeks out of the summer to enjoy the outdoors, too. In the beginning, the camp could accommodate about 130 screaming and joyous kids.

In 1932, the camp was moved to the farm of Dr. C.C. Crouse, near Stahlstown, still before my time. That year, the Greensburg Kiwanis Club built the small infirmary with five cots. In 1949, the Boy Scouts moved on to a new camp called Conestoga and Wesco became a Girl Scout camp. By then, it could accommodate 150 girls from age seven to seventeen and cost sixteen dollars a week.

III

Looking into Somerset County

FLIGHT 93: WRITTEN ON THE WALLS OF THE TEMPORARY MEMORIAL

There is a silence in the fields of Somerset County where the Flight 93 airplane fell from the sky and crashed. The silence is deafening. The silence has been there since the last embers of the hijacked airplane were extinguished and the government declared the area sacred ground. What makes it even more poignant is that the Flight 93 crash was into the heart of rural America. Towns with names like Shanksville, Stoystown and Hemlock Grove and roads like Lambertsville and Buckstown speak of what is good about us. These are places where hardworking Americans till the soil to grow our food, walk into mines to give us fuel and lead simple honorable American lives.

It is enough to say that on September 11, 2001, the United States was attacked by a disgruntled group of foreigners. It was not a country that commanded the attacked. It was not a religion either. It was a group of men and women who believe that Europe and the United States need to stop meddling in the business of others and have caused enormous suffering for the people of the Middle East and western Asia for over two centuries.

Whatever the reason, two planes crashed into the World Trade Center in New York, another hit the Pentagon in Washington D.C. and a third crashed into this open field in rural Pennsylvania, in Somerset County.

Flight 93's temporary memorial. Gigapan image taken in July 2009. *Author's photo.*

Americans were numb. Memorials were planned. Time slowly passed as plans were made. In the meantime, a temporary memorial was erected in the Pennsylvania field. While the temporary memorial was still standing, I picked up my gigapan and camera and went to see and pay my own homage. A gigapan is a robot. You attach a camera to it, attach it to a tripod and place it in front of a panorama you wish to film. The wonder of the gigapan is that, once you decide what image you want to capture, you set the image by telling the gigapan you want to take a certain number of pictures vertically and a certain number horizontally. Once you click start, the robot moves the camera through the vertical and horizontal field and the camera begins to take those pictures. If you picked four by five, it would shoot twenty images.

Then you take the camera home, download your images to a computer and stitch the images together into one searchable, huge picture that is so large it can be placed on the side of a barn like an old mail pouch sign and be crystal clear. Most amazing is that you can zoom into the image and look at the smallest item with clarity: a bird in flight, a flower in a field of weeds or a message on a chain link fence in the Somerset countryside.

Usually one tries to take an image where there is no movement. But it was not possible the day I was at the memorial. The silent visitors where there to pay homage. They moved slowly down the fence, looking and reading what they saw. I was not going to disturb their reverence at all. I was afraid my image would be ruined, but when I processed my work, I found a surreal, emotional portrait that captures not only the items left behind by visitors on the fence, but partial images of the people who came to honor them. The people were fragmented, diffused and disjointed. Those feelings are fitting at such a site. I found my image was not disrespectful but poignant and proper.

The first temporary memorial was a platform with a lecture area and a single chain link fence. As the visitors came to the area, they brought with them their own experiences and left behind reminders of their sorrow and their veneration. Pieces of paper showing their emotions pepper the fence between the flags and bunting: "We will never forget," said one dated February 2, 2008; "May you rise up as eagles," said another written by someone named Whitney; "With a humble heart, I extend to you my sincere respect and honor;" said a third; and "Land of the free, because of the brave" was another. These, and the multitude of other messages, are as much a part of the experience as the memorial itself. They speak of a nation and a world in confusion and mourning.

In addition to the messages, rosaries and crosses dangle from the fence amid myriad hats: red hats, blue hats and hats with military hews, but all in the shape of the very typical American baseball–style hats. Pilgrims from Dallas, New York, Chicago and Santa Ana placed them there. So did someone from the USS *Caron*, the USS *Benner*, a Vietnam Veteran and a fellow worker from United Airlines. Hats are followed by a plethora of license plates from Dover, Seattle, Nevada and more from the military: the USS *Philadelphia* and the USS *Minnesota*.

T-shirts from middle school children with signatures attached, baseballs, a watch, a locket, a spider man doll and even a tin man from the *Wizard of Oz* represent the feelings of the world's youth. These young people, be they American or not, surely do not understand why mankind cannot get along, why grownups do not follow the rules taught to them when they were youths.

One entire section is devoted to badges left by policeman from Miami, San Marino, Munhall, Noblesville, Beloit, Fife, Sacramento and Houston. They came to honor their brothers, their comrades, their heroes. They came from all parts of the country. They left a little bit of themselves behind as a tribute to the few who gave all they had.

Detail of the Flight 93 gigapan, showing hats left by visitors in tribute. *Author's photo*.

Merged into this panorama are a few of the visitors my camera has memorialized: a head in front of a flag, tennis shoes near a small statue of a Madonna, a small boy close beside his father and a woman's ponytail near the stars and stripes. Somehow their disjointed images fit the emotion of the Memorial.

This gigapan is my homage. It is my tribute. It is my way of saying I remember. I honor you. I look for peace in the world. I wish we could all sit down and settle our differences and heal our wounds without violence.

Differences in color, race, religion, nationality and gender have divided us for thousands of years. We have fought each other, maimed each other and destroyed each other. This memorial and the thousands like it around the world stand as witness to man's inhumanity to man. We have made poor progress in understanding each other and working together. Would that we could.

To visit the gigapan online and be able to zoom in and read all the messages and view the insignias go to www.gigapan.info/gigapans/29577.

A MAPLE TREE IS NOT A MAPLE TREE IS NOT A MAPLE TREE

A maple tree is not a maple tree is not a maple tree. Are you surprised? I'm not. There are over one hundred different types of maple trees. There are even some maple trees in Asia that never lose their leaves. Regardless of where they grow, one thing they all have in common is the five-point leaf.

Not all maple trees can produce maple sap. You can't go up to any old maple tree and stab a stick in it to get sap. The red, black and sugar maples are the best for sugaring. The very best is the sugar maple. It is the tallest and also the most flamboyant, as its leaves turn myriad colors in autumn just before falling off.

So what is maple sugar? Just like humans, maple trees get ready for winter by storing starch (our fat). When the cold weather comes, the starch turns to sugar. At night, the sap stays in the roots of the tree, but during the day it travels up the trunk. In the spring, the sugar is sap and can be tapped. But you must leave the kids alone. A tree should be thirty- to forty-years-old before you stick it. It can be tapped until it is about one hundred years old. That is the rest of its lifespan. You can't stick it too often either—no more than three taps per tree, per year, please. For your efforts, you should get about ten gallons of sap from a tree. It takes thirty to fifty gallons of sap to make only one gallon of syrup, so to go commercial, you need a lot of trees. That gallon can weigh up to ten pounds.

The most popular practice is to render the sap into maple syrup. As with everything, there are grades to the syrup: A and B. Then, just to drive you nuts, A is divided again: light amber, medium amber and dark amber. A is used over pancakes, in milk shakes, with sweet potatoes, on ice cream and even on grapefruit. B is for cooking and baking. The sap can also be turned into sugar, but probably only those who live within a sugaring area would use maple sugar cubes. To create sugar, you must boil the sap twice, once to produce the syrup and again to turn the syrup into sugar.

Neither sugar nor syrup is easy to make. It takes a lot of time and patience. It is a cold job, as most of the work is outdoors, and the best temperature to tap a tree is forty degrees. A grove of trees is called a sugar bush. The place where the sap is treated is called a sugarhouse. There, you boil the sap over a wood fire until all the water is gone and it reduces and turns amber in color. That is the syrup. To get the sugar, as noted, you must boil it again.

Maple syrup is a true American product, and we owe its discovery to our Native Americans. They, in turn, learned about the syrup from the animals, mostly squirrels. They call the first full moon in spring the Sugar Moon, for that is when the sap is tapped.

Canada produces a lot of maple syrup, so does Vermont. But the Laurel Highlands has its own, especially in Somerset County. Most of the mapleing in the state happens here. There is even a multi-day festival with a queen, games, great food and, of course, plenty of maple syrup.

The best thing about maple syrup is that it is an all-natural product. That means it is good for you.

IV

Around Westmoreland County

A FRICK OBSERVATORY AND A
BRASHEAR TELESCOPE

Henry Clay Frick grew up in Mount Pleasant. He attended the local schools, bought his penny candy in the local candy stores and went to work in one of the buildings on Main Street. Then, as a young man, he went down the road to Broad Ford along the Youghiogheny to work in his grandfather Overholt's distillery. It was there, in 1871, that the young man turned his face to coal and erected his first mine. By 1894, Henry Clay Frick owned forty-three mines and was a millionaire.

After his success, Frick began his philanthropy to Mount Pleasant. He gave the town a municipal building and then a park, which became Frick Park, and in the midst of the park, he had an observatory built with a revolving roof. That wasn't all. Inside the observatory was an incredible telescope.

The telescope was a Brashear Refractor Telescope that was twelve-feet-tall and six-inches in diameter. The telescope was created by another regional genius—John Brashear. Brashear, born in Brownsville, became one of the most successful producers of telescopes and precision scientific instruments in the world and was head of the Allegheny Observatory in Pittsburgh.

According to the *Outlook*, a magazine of the day, the observatory opened in 1894. Frick placed the observatory in the care of the local school district.

A snippet of a Fowler map of Mount Pleasant, showing the former site of the Frick Observatory in Frick Park. *Courtesy of the Mount Pleasant Area Historical Society.*

But the school district was overwhelmed by the care of such a facility, especially the delicate telescope. Nor did they have such a need. More students from the local institute used it. They, too, could not care for it. In addition, the town became embroiled in a discussion over who owned the park and who had access. Sometime in the spring of 1903, Brashear came to inspect the observatory. In a letter to Frick on June 2, 1903, he complained to Frick:

> *I met members of the Council, School Board and the Principal of the schools, with whom I paid a visit to the park and the observatory. I found the observatory in rather bad condition, because, after its transfer of the park to the city there seemed to be a difference of opinion as to who should take the responsibility of caring for it, with the result that no one cared for it properly. I found also that the brass parts of the instrument were in a curious condition, i.e., A heavy "patina" having formed upon it, which I can account for only on the theory of the great amount of sulphur in the atmosphere, forming a sulphide of zinc on the brass surfaces. This can, I think, be remedied by nickel plating all the brass parts.*[50]

It was the age of coal and coke, and Mount Pleasant was surrounded by no less than ten different mines and thousands of coke ovens. The air was polluted. The brass on the telescope was being destroyed from the coke-oven environment of the area. Brashear was upset. On January 8, 1904, Brashear told Frick he had taken back the neglected telescope and repaired the observatory building.

He noted: "I cannot refrain from saying that the authorities of Mount Pleasant were shamefully neglectful of your gift, and I confess I considered it almost sacrilege to see the condition of the instrument, with many of the parts gone and the rest not cared for."[51] For overhauling the telescope, Brashear billed Frick $340.75. It is believed that the telescope was never returned to Mount Pleasant.

Where did the telescope go? At first, Glenn A. Walsh of Friends of the Zeiss and Bart Fried of the Antique Telescope Society deduced, in an Internet discussion, that the telescope was in Vermont. Fried believed that, in 1915, the Mount Pleasant telescope was given to the Peabody Institute of Salem, Massachusetts. There, too, it remained mostly unused, as they kept it in the basement. In 1939, it was sent on to Phillips Academy in Andover, Massachusetts. In 2003, the academy gave it to John Briggs, who sold it to astronomy aficionado Matt Considine of Vermont in 2005. But that telescope does not show evidence of the brass being coated by nickel and does not have the nameplate of John Brashear that appeared on the Mount Pleasant telescope on its completion. This suggests a much more recent origin. Back to square one. Where is the Mount Pleasant telescope? We may never know.

As for Frick Park, it is still there. The observatory is gone. A portion of the park was used to erect an armory, also gone. The giant trees that rimmed the parameter were cut down in 2013. But daily, the air is filled with the laughter of children who play ball and run around the edges teasing the dogs that are being walked by their owners.

FINNS IN MONESSEN

It's called Finntown! That's its name! It has been in existence as long as Monessen has been a city. That's 116 years. It is obvious who lived there, Finns: immigrants from Finland who came to the United States around the turn of the twentieth century. The first Finns were in Monessen in 1897 as the

Finnish Hall on Fourth Street in Monessen. *Courtesy of the author.*

mills that would make the city famous were being erected and the immigrants who would fill the jobs were crossing the ocean. By 1906, 900 Finns were living in the small boomtown, most of them working in William Donner's tin mill. As with all the other immigrants in this amazing melting pot of nearly thirty different nationalities, the Finns congregated around a cluster of streets they would call their own. It was there, in Finntown, situated along Motheral, Chestnut, Clarendon and Knox Avenues, crossed by Fourth and Sixth Streets, that the Finnish community grew into 1,600 souls.

It wasn't long before the community began to turn the streets into a mirage of their lives back in Finland. They established two social centers. Along Fourth Street, anchoring one end of the community was the Finnish Temperance Hall, also called the White Finn Hall. Along Sixth Street, anchoring the other end of the community was the Socialist Hall, the Red Finn Hall. The two halls defined the two moral and political views of the inhabitants.

The Finns were further divided by the Sampo and Osmo Cooperatives, which brought Finnish goods into the community. In these stores, the Finns would shop for lingonberries for rice pudding, herring that they ate with sour cream, *lipia kala* (dried cod) for Christmas and cardamom to make the wonderful Finnish *niswa* bread. A "red" Finn shopped at Sampos, a "white" at Osmo. There was also a Finnish bakery (owned by Jacob Knuuttila), a barbershop (owned by John Hikkinin), a confectionary

The world-famous Louhi Band preparing for another journey. *Courtesy of the author.*

(owned by Ohota) and a clothing store (owned by F.W. Nahi) in Finntown. If you wanted a sauna in Monessen, you had to go to Finntown, that is, if you knew what a sauna was. If you wanted to listen to good music, you would sit on the lawns of the homes around Fourth Street on a Sunday morning and listen to the world-famous Louhi Band. The music filled the air for blocks around, and families would open their windows or sit on their porches to enjoy the free concerts during rehearsals. Not only did the Louhi Band play music for Monessen—marching at the head of most parades and giving concerts at the high school and city park—they went abroad where they performed for the King of Finland and marched in New York City parades. The Louhi Band won every competition it entered. The Louhi Band was a world-class musical group that made every citizen of Monessen proud.

The music filtered into the schools where Finnish children were trained by the Louhi Band program comprised most of the high school band. The Finns were great contributors to the growth of Monessen. Out of the success of the Louhi Band was born the Sibelius Club, an organization that held the rights to distribute the music of Sibelius throughout the United States. As the Finnish residents began leaving Monessen, more and more Italians and Slavs joined the band. World War II brought it to an end.

There were other Finns who have made their mark on the community and the world. Dr. Christian Anfinsen, formerly of Finntown, won the Nobel Prize in Chemistry in 1972. Blanche Thebom was a famous mezzo-soprano who performed for years at the Metropolitan Opera in New York City and went on to teach voice and direct opera programs.

Thirteen Finns from Monessen were on the *Titanic* that fateful April night as the unsinkable ship slipped into the cold, harsh waters of the North Atlantic. Four more Monessenites—Hungarians—were supposed to have been aboard, too, but escaped the fated voyage because of sickness. They were lucky. The Finnish community was deeply affected by the tragedy. Only five of the travelers made it home. The two boarding houses at 400 and 401 Motheral Avenue were hushed in silence in respect for the people who did not arrive.

Like the rest of the community, World War I, the Strike of 1919 and the terror of the Palmer Raids pushed a number of Finns to leave the states. Some went home; others went to Russia. By 1930, the tin mill fell victim to the Depression and more Finns left. Today, a small group of Finns is struggling to maintain their identity in the community. A few years ago, they closed the Finnish church, which had opened in 1902. Yet Monessen's Finns, even in diminished numbers, are still making history. The Unknown Child, recently identified by DNA in the Halifax cemetery for victims of the *Titanic*, was first thought to be the youngest Panula child, Eino (more about him in the next story).

MONESSEN AND THE *TITANIC*

Seventeen people listed Monessen, Pennsylvania, as their final destination on the HMS *Titanic* passenger lists in 1912. Most were Finnish immigrants. Most survived, but a few met their death in the icy waters of the North Atlantic on that fateful night. Most of the dead came from a single family. Here are the men and women bound for Monessen on the *Titanic*.

Helga Lindquist Hirvonen, age twenty-two, her two-year-old daughter, Hildur, and her brother Eino Lindquist, a twenty-year-old laborer, were bound for 400 Motheral Avenue in a section of Monessen that had become known as Finntown. Thirty-two-year-old Erik Jussila, on his way to 482 Motheral Avenue, was traveling by himself. Also headed for Motheral Avenue, this time at 401, were the newly married couple Pekka and Elin Hakkarainen. Twenty-eight-year-old Pekka had immigrated to Monessen several years before the disaster. He worked as a tinsmith in the tin mill. He had returned to Finland for a visit and was returning with his new bride, Elin, who had also been in America before.

Bound ultimately for Coal Center, Pennsylvania, but ending their official *Titanic* journey in Monessen, were Maria Panula, her five children, Juho, Ernesti, Eino, Urho and Jaako, and a companion, Sanni Riihivuori. Maria and her husband, John, owned a farm, and she had returned to Finland to sell their property there and return to the United States.

Four more passengers destined for Monessen were scheduled to be on the *Titanic*. They were refused passage because of a childish prank that left one of the children with an open wound. They were not Finnish. They were a Hungarian mother and her children on their way to meet their patriarch in Monessen. He worked for the Pittsburgh Steel Company.

That brings the total number to seventeen! That is an incredible number for a town with a population of twelve thousand.

The Ship

The HMS *Titanic* was hailed as the unsinkable ship. She was on her maiden voyage out of Southampton, bound for New York. The passengers were divided into first class, second class and third class (steerage). Our Monessen passengers were traveling in steerage, as most of the immigrants to American did.

On April 15, 1912, the unsinkable ship hit an iceberg in the North Atlantic and sank. The crew and passengers were totally unprepared for such an event. There were over 2,000 people on board and too few lifeboats by half. Only 705 people were rescued, and over 1,500 drowned or froze to death in the cold North Atlantic waters.

Through local newspaper interviews, residents of Monessen and the Mon Valley told first-hand accounts of the events aboard the *Titanic* that dreadful night. It is an amazing and horrifying tale.

When the Ship Hit the Iceberg

Most of our travelers were tucked into bed in their cabins when the ship struck the iceberg. On April 23, 1912, the account of Helga Lindquist Hirvonen appeared in the *Charleroi Mail*, the newspaper of the small town across the river from Monessen.

Most of the third cabin passengers were awakened I guess about midnight on that last Sunday. Grabbing whatever clothing they could they rushed forth. They were met by officers of the ship who said "Get back to your places; there's nothing wrong." All went back. However, there was considerable excitement.

Erik Jussila was in his cabin in the bow of the ship. His friend John Niskanen said to him, "*Nouse yl s kuolematas katsomaan*"—get up and see your death.

Maria Panula's family was scattered from the bow to the stern. She searched the ship for her children. The oldest, Ernesti, sixteen and Jaako, fourteen, had been ordered to the bow with the single men, while Maria and the remaining children, Juho, Urho and Eino, were at the stern. She did not want it that way, but that is how the crew split her family. Sanni Riihivuori, twenty-two, also going to Coal Center, and Anna Turja, eighteen, a neighbor from Finland, were also in steerage.

Escaping Steerage

In an interview by the *Monessen Daily Independent*, Eino Lindquist remembered: "I was a passenger in the third cabin and had been in bed about 2 hours when my room mate and I were awakened by people running to and fro on the deck. We hurriedly dressed ourselves and put on our heaviest clothes and our overcoats, the night being very damp and cold."

Helga Hirvonen remembered:

Some time later—I don't know how long—it seemed that the big steamer was tilting. Then there was another rush from the promenade deck. The officers couldn't drive us back then. After some time there came a shout for the women to come up on another deck. Some of us understood and started…There was great confusion and a babble of tongues. Many of the third cabin passengers could not understand English and didn't know what was being shouted to them. The rest of us were too badly frightened and excited I suppose, to help them much and as a result half of women and children and a majority of the men did not get away from the steerage at all.

Elin Hakkarainen was one of the steerage passengers who owe their survival to the stewards who helped them. She related the story to her family, who published it in a book called *I'm Going to see What Has Happened: The Personal Experience of 3rd Class Finnish Titanic Survivor, Mrs. Elin Hakkarainen.*

> *The door at the end of the passageway was locked! I ran to the other end of the passageway and found the door locked also. After a bit of wandering I discovered another door which was unlocked and led to another passageway. I finally ran into my friend who had awakened me. A ship's steward appeared with a small group of women saying "You better come with us." He said, "There is another way to get to the upper deck." He directed us to a service ladder, which was used only by the crew to get around the ship. "Follow me," said the steward, "We do not have much time." We went up the ladder, through the second class dining room, up another flight of stairs to the second class promenade and finally up to the boat deck.*

Entering the Lifeboats

The rule at the lifeboats was women and children first. It must have been horrifically chaotic. Not everyone remembered the events the same way. Helga Hirvonen remembers getting safely aboard the lifeboats one way: "I was the last to be given a place on the last lifeboat. I was very carefully picked up because I had my baby with me. Mrs. Ajkarainen [Hakkarainen] was seized by the neck and foot, I believe, and tossed into a life boat. She fainted."

Elin Hakkarainen remembered the ordeal another way:

> *As our group of women huddled against a deck house, an officer motioned for us to get into a lifeboat that was being loaded. I didn't move, for I was still scanning the faces in order to locate Pekka. The lifeboat was being guarded by the ship officers standing in a semi-circle around it. Occasionally a man would try to get through the circle, but would be scared off by the officers' pistols. There was a lot of cursing and yelling from one group of men. In fact, they were fighting amongst themselves. One of the officers pointed at me saying, "Room for one more, lady. Come on. Hurry!" As I stepped into the lifeboat, it was already moving downward. I lost my balance, almost falling between*

the lifeboat and ship until someone in the lifeboat grabbed my arm and pulled me into a seat. On the way down we stopped at a lower deck and picked up one more lady. As the lifeboat continued its descent, the stern of the Titanic rose higher and higher. We wondered if the ropes lowering the lifeboats would be long enough to reach the water.

Helga Hirvonen remembered Pekka helping Elin into the boat, "Her husband bade her a fond goodbye. He intended to get into a life boat, but heroically gave way to others."

Helga's brother Eino remembered it too: "Not realizing the extreme danger I was in at the time, I wandered around for about half an hour and came upon Mr. Hakkarainen who had just aided in putting his bride of three months into one of the boats." Elin did not remember this.

As for the Panula family, we find more conflicting stories. According to Anna, one of the older boys came to tell them the ship was sinking. They headed to the boat deck. They got separated, but Anna saw Mrs. Panula on the boat deck. She was hysterical. Ironically, Mrs. Panula had lost a child before she started on this journey to America. He had drowned!

Helga Hirvonen also saw Maria Panula. She reported, "One of the last persons I saw before leaving was Mrs. John Paluna [sic]. I knew her well, she was so much confused that, poor woman, she hardly knew which way to turn. She was one of the last to come on deck. I presume she was trying to collect her family. None of them escaped."

John Panula, back in Coal Center, waited until April 21 to find out what had happened to his family. He reported to the *Charleroi Mail*:

I had a good farm in Finland. My wife and I had been there about three years, then I started for our former home in America, she to follow me later with our children. The last word I heard was that she was leaving Finland…My farm was sold, I guess it was for $4,000. My wife was bringing $2,000 of this with her. Now everything is gone.

The Ordeal of the Men

Eino Lindquist continued his story: "Going out on the deck we saw the sailors lowering the lifeboats away, filled with women, with men at each end and in the middle to guide and row. My friend, Jussila was called upon to help row one of the boats and I was left alone on the deck." The last comment about Eric Jussila is very important, as the man was accused of jumping into the boats in order to save himself. Perhaps we will never know what truly happened, but Eino's comments are in Jussila's favor.

Eino and Pekka were still on board the *Titanic* as it went through its final shutters before sinking into the sea. Eino continued his story:

> *Together we watched until the last boat put off and saw many of the men who had been left on board make a vain effort to find a place on it but they were clubbed by the sailors in charge and some fell to a watery grave before the ship took its final plunge. It was not long after the last boat had left that we began to realize the situation and then we began to look around for some avenue of escape when suddenly with a deafening sound the boilers blew up, the ship gave one final heave and sank slowly. Many of the men were crying pitifully and the wild chant of their wails could be heard above the lashings of the sea and the grinding crunch of the already splintering hull. The band was not playing when the ship sank or else I did not hear it but I did hear the pianos in the first and second cabins. Being on the third deck our section reached the level of the sea before that of the first and second cabins and the waves washed Mr. Hakkarainen and I into the ocean and the last words he said were, "Good Bye." Being a fairly good swimmer I exerted myself to the utmost and was able to reach the last life boat which was about 200 yards from where the ship went down and was taken on board.*

Watching the Ship Sink

Most of us have images of the *Titanic* sinking into the sea. That is from several movies and a number of TV shows. But Helga and Elin were there and this is what they had to say. Helga reported:

> *I suppose we had been away from the Titanic twenty minutes when it went down. I saw it plainly. When it took its final dive people were leaping from all sides into the water. Some of them were saved. When our lifeboat left the Titanic's side it was only about half filled. It wasn't long however, before we picked up enough to completely fill it. My brother was found on a raft after we had been six and a half hours at sea.*

Elin offers an even more graphic view:

The scene that I now witnessed was forever etched in my memory. I would never forget the sounds that came from the Titanic at this time. As the stern of the ship rose higher and higher, everything within the ship broke loose and went crashing downward to the bow. There was a mad rush of passengers and crew to the rear of the well and poop decks. There seemed to be a mad rush of people from below. The locked doors that I had encountered must have been opened at the last moment. Many hundreds more must have been trapped below decks and crushed by the breaking up of the ship. One of the giant funnels toppled to the deck crushing many passengers as it slid into the water. The screaming and moaning of the trapped passengers was beyond description. The Titanic was standing straight up, the three huge propellers glistened in the starlight. We were all hypnotized by the sight of the giant ship standing on end, going down slowly, ever so slowly, as if an invisible hand was holding it back. Hundreds of people were holding on to the railings, stairs and ladders, capstans and framework of the rear docking bridge. The ship's lights, which had remained on during the entire episode, finally went out.

The Survivors

So, who survived? Helga and her daughter, her brother Eino, Eric and Elin made it into the lifeboats, endured the journey in the rescue ship *Carpathia* to New York, were cared for by the Red Cross and given tickets to Monessen. Pekka, the newlywed, did not survive. He died in the cold waters of the North Atlantic. What of the Panulas? None of them made it off the *Titanic*. They should have because, as it is obvious, the rule was women and children first. But poor Mrs. Panula could not manage to keep her family together and kept wandering around. It cost them their lives. Also lost was Sanni Riihivuori, who was traveling with them.

Monessen Hears of the Tragedy

The first headlines in Monessen lamented the loss of John Linja, a doubler in Mill No. 12 of the tin mill. He was listed as one of the passengers. The rumor spread throughout Monessen that John, and his entire family, was lost. In fact, he was not on the *Titanic*.

The train station in Monessen where the *Titanic* survivors arrived after their ordeal. *Courtesy of the author.*

On April 19, four days after the tragedy, Matt Hirvonen got a telegram that his wife, Helga Lindquist Hirvonen, and their daughter were safe, but the remainder of the Monessen-bound Finns had probably drowned.

But on April 22, five *Titanic* survivors reached Monessen on the 9:00 a.m. express train. The banner headline in the *Monessen Daily Independent* read, "Bride of Three Months Widowed—Entire party in a Highly Nervous State—Band Did Not Play as Ship Sank—Men Cried Pitifully But Died Bravely."

The Hungarians

What of the Hungarians? On April 11, 1912, Mary Torkos's mischievous brother Michael pushed her onto a rock pile, and she scratched and bruised her face. When the family arrived at the *Titanic* the next day, the officers refused to board them. Mary's scratches could become infected, and they refused to allow her on board. They set sail from Southampton a few days later on the *Titanic*'s sister ship, the *Kortland*.

While the family was making a terrifying Atlantic crossing, their father, Joseph, was working as a wirepuller at Pittsburgh Steel in Monessen. He had received a

119

letter from his family that they were to sail on the *Titanic*. When he heard that the *Titanic* sank, he presumed his family was lost. What a burden he carried.

The family arrived in Monessen late at night and did not have Joseph's address, as he was living in a boarding house. So, they stopped a stranger on the street for help. He took them to Pittsburgh Steel, and as luck would have it, Joseph was working. At first, he refused to come to the office. He told them, "You have the wrong person, my family was all lost on the *Titanic*."

MONESSEN'S ITALIANS: FIGHTING FOR THE DREAM

The landscape in Monessen still holds the occasional Italian vegetable garden. They are not hard to spot. The old windowpanes that serve as hothouses for herbs and flat-leaved parsley give them away, as do the splintered wooden poles and old kitchen rags that hold up the tomato vines. The nostalgic scene takes us back to the early twentieth century, when the tone and fabric of the Italian American community was forming in Monessen.

The Italian community was never as cohesive as the Italian garden. Everyone who knows anything about Italians knows the community was segregated. The divisions were sharply defined when the vegetable gardens were abundant and the wooden poles not quite so grey. Southern Italians, from Abruzzi to Sicily, with names ending in *o*'s and *a*'s like DeRocco,* Dalfonso and Panapinto, lived around Morgan and Schoonmaker Avenues. Both streets overlooked the smoke and stench of the Pittsburgh Steel Company. If there was a single bit of space anywhere in that neighborhood, someone planted a fig tree. The women cooked southern specialties like Sicilian *aranchini* or Abruzzese *maccheroni alla chitarra*. For their wine, they enjoyed cooking with bittersweet, pungent Marsala. In their music, the southern Italians in Monessen enjoyed *festa* bands that played happy music with accordions and mandolins. Their club was the Italian Society of Mutual Aid.

Northern Italians, from Tuscany to the Piedmont, with names like Viviani, Guiducci and Parigi, were not quite as lively. They lived around Knox

---

* The spelling of the Italian names may differ from how they are spelled today. Most were taken directly from the Polk's *Monessen County Directory of 1924–25*.

Northern Italian men at the NIPA hall in Monessen. *Courtesy of the author.*

Avenue and Chestnut Street and Ninth and Fourth Streets, on the fringes of Finntown. There wasn't a northern garden that did not have a sage bush where, summer or winter, someone would run out to clip a few fragrant leaves to roast a chicken or grill a pork chop. They did not celebrate Christmas Eve with seven fishes either. They had never heard of it. They enjoyed their music brassy and liked the brass bands with horns and trombones. Most of them spoke a Tuscan dialect, which made it easier to understand each other, but difficult to understand the good folks on Morgan or Schoonmaker Avenues. Among the northern wine specialties was *Vin Santo*, made from grapes that were first turned to raisins by tacking them to cellar rafters to age. These Italians belonged to the NIPA, the Northern Italian Political Association.

Even their grocers serviced different needs. Armedeo Auselivi on Chestnut Street, Dominic Coccari on Knox Avenue and Tarnquillo Dreucci on Fourth Street catered to the northerners who wanted butter, chestnuts and Parmesan cheese. Louis Imbrogno and George Severino on Morgan Avenue sold to the southerners who were looking for pine nuts, raisins and mozzarella.

To the city, an Italian was an Italian, but as every ethnic group knew, your village and your region were far more important that your nationality. When the Liberty Bond Drives of World War I raged in the city around 1818, each

The façade of Italian Hall in Monessen, the club of the southern Italians. *Author's photo.*

ethnic group tried to outdo the other to prove their Americanism. Within the Italian community, it was a battle to see which group, the southerners or the northerners, would buy the most bonds, give the most soldiers to the war effort or have more members in the marching band. Even the creation of their clubs was a rivalry.

Legend maintains that the earliest Italians in Monessen were mostly northerners. Those early immigrants helped create the skyline of the city and placed their first clubhouse at 601 Third Street. There, as in Italy, the northerners ruled. In 1907, four hundred more Italians came to the community to erect the open-hearth furnaces of Pittsburgh Steel. The balance of power began to shift. At one disrupted meeting, the northerners were outvoted by the southerners and simply walked out and founded their own club in their own neighborhood: the NIPA, on Knox Avenue. The Mutual Aid retaliated by building the New Italian Hall on the main street of town and made it one story higher than the NIPA. The divisions were firmly in place. This was

A blackball machine used to vote on new members. One black ball meant no membership. *Author's photo.*

in 1913. In 1950, a businesswoman was blackballed by the NIPA's lady's association because she was not Northern Italian.

Rivalry aside, when it came time to face the larger community, the Italians stuck together. Sometimes. The power in the community belonged to the earlier immigrants: the Germans, Scots, Irish and Welsh owned the businesses, newspapers and the mills. Considering themselves Americans, they believed the central and southern Europeans were foreigners. The African Americans were the least respected of all. The three groups fought against—and occasionally with—each other in reaching for the American dream. Each of Monessen's many ethnic factions had their own stores and worked in specific departments in the mills. The Italians were no different. The southerners worked mostly in the rod mills. The northerners worked mostly in the labor gang because the boss in the labor gang was a northern Italian named Dominic "Manco" Bindi.

Nothing better illustrates the disparity in ethnic employment at Pittsburgh Steel—and mills like it in Monessen and across southwestern Pennsylvania— than the wage scale people were paid. A native-born worker earned $17.81 a week at Pittsburgh Steel in 1919. Native born blacks earned $14.82. A native-born of a foreign father earned anywhere from $20.79 to $12.77. For the immigrants who had just arrived, the English ($18.80), Scots ($19.01) and Welsh ($22.15) immigrants earned the most, with the Slovenians ($11.89), northern Italians ($12.01), southern Italians ($11.83) and Greeks ($11.85) earning the least. Even in the mills, the southerners came last.

In their neighborhoods, be they northern or southern, the Italians were free to develop their entrepreneurial skills as they wished. Small mom and pop stores flourished enough to support families, a task almost impossible today. By 1925, there were nine fruit stores in Monessen, half were Italian—including Thomas Parnella, Joseph Parnella and Salvatore Parnella at 243, 245 and 247 Schoonmaker Avenue, respectively. Of the five bakeries in Monessen, Italians went to Fontanelli's at 436 Donner Avenue if they wanted biscotti or crusty bread. There were eight Italian barbers, none singing: Cardelli, Cardelle, Cocchiara, D'Errico, Garofola, La Brosse, Lapresto and Parnella. Coal haulers included Art Moncini, who became a beer distributor, and Marshall Brighenti, who owned Victoria Coal.

Entrepreneurial skills opened the door to all types of industry. Sources maintain that there was no mafia in Monessen. There were a few black hands who extorted money from their own people. There definitely was prostitution and gambling, which played a dominant role in Monessen, from its founding to the 1970s. It was mostly run by Italians and was big enough to bring national attention in the 1950s with a *Collier's* magazine article. "Operation Crusade," led by a Methodist minister, rocked all of southwestern Pennsylvania's vice and almost succeeded in ending decades of tolerated crime in Monessen. Almost.

There were no mill owners with Italian names, no medical doctors, no dentists, jewelers, teachers, hoteliers, insurance salesmen, electricians or plumbers—not in the first generation of immigrants. One of the few Italian commercial enterprises was a printer, John Fiorilli, at 406 Knox Avenue. There were Italian tailors: Nick Forty, Pasquale Martucci, Frank Scalise and Adamo Visca. There were Italian musicians and music teachers: John Jannotta, Frank Rizzuto and Frank Lombardo. Monessen even had an Italian stonecutter for monuments: the Bianchi family. Almost every shoemaker in Monessen was an Italian: Joseph Greco, Dominick Persico, Anthony Pilleuggi, Salvatore Sparacino and Rudolph Trilli, and this was just 1925.

Monessen and its Italian community thrived. People got paid here and spent their money here. That doesn't happen today throughout small town America. The Italians came slowly together. One reason was the schools.

In the 1920–30s there were 4,645 students enrolled in Monessen schools, representing twenty-seven different nationalities. The largest groups were 940 Americans, 837 Italians, 727 Slavs and 486 Carpatho-Rusyns. The children, bound together by the American language and by the epithets "wop" or "dago" learned to cope. The church was the next cohesive institution. The Catholic Italians, almost 95 percent of the Italians in Monessen, went to the single Italian Catholic church, Saint Cajetans. Yet even it was keenly aware of the differences of its congregation. In 1949, when the new Saint Cajetans Church was dedicated on Knox Avenue, the commemorative booklet announced there were 3,500 Italians in Monessen and felt it necessary to break them into regions by most membership: Abruzzi, Calabria, Sicily, Apulia, Campania and the north. The northerners were on the wane.

Today, Morgan Avenue is a state of mind. Not only did the people move to more affluent neighborhoods, but the street itself was wiped away by redevelopment in the 1970s. The people miss it so much they hold reunions. The northern neighborhoods are gone too. Children, educated by the backbreaking dollars from the mills, left and never looked back.

But the Italian legacy in Monessen is a proud one. One of the most famous Italian Americans in the state was Hugo J. Parente, mayor of Monessen for over twenty years. Louis Manderino became a justice on the supreme court of Pennsylvania, while his brother Jimmy Manderino was speaker of the Pennsylvania legislature. From asphalt companies to builders, educators, lawyers, architects and musicians, the sons and daughters of Monessen's Italian American community are making a difference in the world. Isn't that the dream their parents and grandparents fought the mills, the Americans and each other to give them?

Could Rebuilding the Infrastructure of America Have Saved the Steel Industry?

If you ask the former steelworkers in Monessen, a small steel town along the banks of the Monongahela River south of Pittsburgh, you will get a resounding "yes!"

Monessen was one of the speculative towns created by Pittsburgh tycoons at the turn of the nineteenth century. Its major streets honor their names: Donner, Schoonmaker, McKee, Reed and Knox. From its birth in 1898, its purpose was industrial, and no less than three major mills lined the river for

Unique dual cast house and blast furnaces of the Pittsburgh Steel Company. Now gone. *Courtesy of the author.*

over three miles: the American Sheet and Tin Plate, Page's Wire and Fence and Pittsburgh Steel.

The laborers in these mills were immigrants. The "tin mill" brought the Finnish community to town. The other two mills were populated with a bevy of nationalities, mostly from central and southern Europe, who lived in pockets of the community and worked in clusters in the various mill departments: Croatians, Slavs, Poles, Ukrainians, Carpatho-Rusyns, Hungarians, Greeks, Italians, Syrians, Germans and African Americans. They had their own churches, their own clubs and their own histories in the community. Monessen was a true American "melting pot."

The tin mill closed in the 1930s, but the other two mills thrived, contributing wire to the Golden Gate Bridge, steel for Chrysler and, during World War II, became part of the "Arsenal for Democracy" as ton after ton of steel went into tanks, planes, landing strips and even bombs and bullets.

At its peak, Monessen had over twenty-five thousand people and Pittsburgh Steel employed over ten thousand valley men and women. But in 1950, the steel mill closed its fence, nail and barbed wire production. In 1966, with the import of rods at nearly 50 percent of the market value, the welded-wire mill and the Rod Mill closed. Then, in 1968, Pittsburgh Steel merged with Wheeling Steel to form Wheeling–Pittsburgh Steel (W-P), a move that would eventually bring Monessen down.

So, by the 1970s, steel was in trouble. Labor costs were high. Imports were undercutting the industry. Automation was cutting jobs. Page's closed for good in 1972. Of the three major industries in Monessen, only W-P was left standing. Ten thousand people remained in the community and only 2,800 workers lingered in the steel mill. By 1978, W-P had to apply air pollution controls that cost $28.5 million and sent the already shaky finances into the pits.

It was at this time that Dennis Carney became head of W-P Steel. Carney, a Mon Valley boy, was loved and hated. He was flamboyant. He was blunt. He was hard to like. But he had a vision. The country's bridges needed repaired. The dams needed to be reinforced. New rails were needed for the railroads. Even the nation's roadways needed to be overhauled. Dennis Carney saw that the infrastructure of America was old and crumbling. He foresaw the time when it would have to be rebuilt. America would need steel for building, for reinforcing, for rails and for all types of structures. He wanted Pittsburgh Steel to lead the way.

But he needed money. He asked the EPA to extend the payments for the pollution bill. Then he did one more thing: he contracted with the workers to buy preferred stock in the company. They became stockholders, an unprecedented move that would have ramifications throughout the industrial world for years to come. But first, the industry laughed. But Monessen rallied. The workers bought $8.6 million worth of stock. The rest of the industry went apoplectic.

With funds in hand, Carney went to Washington, D.C. and came home with 90 percent of the funding needed for his grand vision: the Economic Development Administration (EDA) and the Farmers Home Loan Administration would cover the cost. The Carter administration agreed to cut foreign imports and work to rebuild the infrastructure of America. Carney achieved what no one else seemed to do: cooperation between management, workers and government.

He built a continuous caster to produce the blooms that were needed for his expanded vision. The workers took even more cuts in salary and benefits. The EPA agreed to extend the pollution payments. Once all was in place, Carney built the rail mill in Monessen. By 1981, everything was ready. W-P Steel was hiring. The orders were coming in. Rails and structural steel were being made.

Wheeling–Pittsburgh Steel was the darling of the *New York Times*, which in article after article, praised the efforts in the small town along the Mon. The *Pittsburgh Business Times* awarded its Enterprise Award to Carney in 1983.

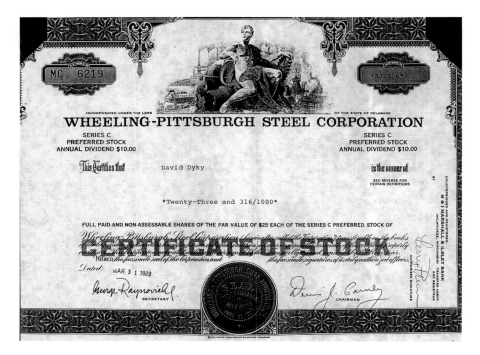

A stock certificate issued by Wheeling–Pittsburgh Steel to its workers. *Courtesy of Dave Dyky.*

The big steel companies were so furious with Carney and his dealings with labor that they banished W-P from their midst.

But Jimmy Carter lost the election in 1980, and Ronald Reagan took office in 1981. The Reagan administration was not eager to save the steel industry or to curtail foreign imports. Nor did it see the need to begin to rebuild the infrastructure of America. It was called Reganomics.

By 1985, Carney's world was falling apart. Steel was not in demand. Prices were crashing. American mills could not compete with foreign imports. The big mills like Jones and Laughlin and the famous Homestead Works were closing. W-P Steel filed for bankruptcy. The men in Monessen were losing patience. They went on a ninety-eight-day strike. It was a catastrophe. They marched. They shouted slogans. They turned against Carney in a move welcomed by their Wheeling brothers, who had been battling to save their own mills. In the fall of 1985, Dennis Carney, Monessen's last hope, resigned. It opened the door for Wheeling to gain control of the company. It did not take long.

Demolition of Blast Furnace Alley. *Author's photo.*

In January 1986, the three rolling mills in the Monessen plant were permanently closed, as was the sinter plant. The entire Monessen plant was closed temporarily in June. By that time, the work force was down to 870. The Jane blast furnace closed permanently in 1986. So did the Basic Oxygen Furnace, the BOF.

The state-of-the-art rail mill, the hope of Monessen (and perhaps the nation), was closed permanently in March 1987. One of the most modern mills in the United States was out of business while the Wheeling plant remained open. In August, a bit of management skullduggery took place: in a single day, the Pittsburgh headquarters of W-P were shut down and moved to Wheeling.

On that morning, Ray Johnson, a Monessen man who was once the boss of the blast furnace area, reported to Pittsburgh for his job as a public relations man and was told to clean everything out of his office because the company was moving that very day. He asked what he should do with the Monessen documents. He was told to throw them away. He did—right into the trunk of his car. Much of what he saved is now deposited at the Monessen Heritage Museum.

The EDA was the major holder of the debt, and they put the rail mill and its surrounding properties up for sale. Locals wanted to buy the Monessen plant and run it themselves, but it was sold to its prime competitor, Bethlehem Steel Company in eastern Pennsylvania. Bethlehem locked the rail mill, posted a guard and threw away the key. It never reopened. Even when the local historical society wanted to use the beautiful Georgian-style office building, erected in the early twentieth century as a museum, Bethlehem refused and had it torn down. Bethlehem wanted the story of steel to be told in Bethlehem, not in Pittsburgh where the giant mills of history resided. They got what they wanted.

Today the Monessen Plant has been razed. The community population is under 7,500. Mostly senior citizens live in houses that need repairs, streets that need repaving and a downtown with buildings about to collapse. The river front has never been redeveloped to its full potential, and generally poor leadership has done little to bring it back, including turning down the Carnegie-Mellon University's Heinz College of Public Policy and Management's offer to assist the community in its redevelopment.

My question to you is: If the Reagan administration was as wise as the Carter administration when it came to steel, could the industry have been saved and would rebuilding the infrastructure of America in the 1980s and '90s have saved thousands and thousands of jobs in a plethora of industries around the country?

A MOUNT PLEASANT HERO

The Congressional Medal of Honor (MOH) is the highest honor the United States can bestow upon a citizen. Since its inception during the Civil War, only 3,425 medals have been awarded. Most states have well under 100 recipients; but Pennsylvania, one of the original thirteen colonies, has 378. Only New York has more. That is very rarified air. One does not win a MOH; one earns it. There are tough guidelines to this honor: proof that the event actually happened, at least two eyewitnesses to authenticate the act of valor, the act goes far beyond the call of duty and evidence that the person risked his or her life.

Therefore, it is a great honor when a community can say with pride, "We have a Medal of Honor winner." Well, Mount Pleasant, Pennsylvania, can make that claim. Even more exciting is the fact that the medal was earned for valor in one of the most famous battles on the American continent—the Battle of the Little Big Horn.

Gray-eyed, brown-haired, five-foot, nine-inch Henry W.B. Mechlin* was a blacksmith in Mount Pleasant. When he left to join the army, he was seconded to a blacksmith company, Company H of the now famous Seventh United States Calvary. The commander of the Seventh was General George Armstrong Custer. His fellow officers were Major Marcus Reno and Captain Frederick Benteen. The quartermasters, including Mechlin, were assigned to Benteen's command.

On June 26, 1876, while pursuing the enemy in Dakota Territory, a group of men was assigned to gather water. The river, the Little Big Horn, was in the hands of the Native Americans and their leaders: Sitting Bull, Crazy Horse and braves from the Sioux and Cheyenne nations. Four of Benteen's soldiers volunteered to cover eleven other soldiers as they drew water from what is now called the Water Carrier Ravine. On August 29, 1878, two years after the event, all fifteen men were awarded the MOH for their bravery. Mechlin's read: "With three comrades, during the entire engagement, courageously held a position that secured water for the command, in the Little Big Horn River fight."

Henry Mechlin did not end his military career after the Battle of the Little Big Horn. He remained in the army and served with distinction in a number of Indian Campaigns, including the Yellowstone and Nez Perce Campaigns of 1877, the Expedition against the Northern Cheyenne in 1878 and the Black Hills Campaign in 1879.

The Yellowstone and Nez Perce Campaigns of 1877 began when the United States government opened the territory to western expansion. The Nez Perce were forced to leave. They fought on for a while, but could not counter the power of the First United States Cavalry under generals Howard, Sturgis and Miles. After the 750 men, women and children retreated over one thousand miles through and beyond what is now Yellowstone National Park, Chief Joseph said the immortal words, "I will fight no more forever." His people were starving. Their children were freezing to death. Henry Mechlin was there at that moment in history.

A year later, Henry Mechlin was with the army as it battled the Cheyenne nation in what is called the Expedition against the Northern Cheyenne in 1878. By that date, many of the Cheyenne nation were already placed on land in Oklahoma. But Chief Dull Knife, along with chiefs Wild Hog and

---

* Henry's last name has been spelled Mechling and Mechlin. I have chosen to use the name Mechlin because it is on the back of his Medal of Honor.

Little Wolf, 89 braves and 146 women and children escaped on September 9, 1878, and headed north. They were headed to Dakota Territory and freedom. Henry Mechlin and the United States Army were in pursuit. All the Cheyenne were killed and fifty soldiers were lost.

After the Black Hills Campaign in 1879, Mechlin finished his five-year term of duty in August 1880. Four years after Big Horn, he came home. One wonders what his thoughts were about all the battles he was in. He wrote about Big Horn, but I have not found anything about the other battles. He was discharged on August 4, 1880. At the request of the military, he returned to the battlefield in 1902. By then, the battlefield had become the Little Bighorn Battlefield National Monument, and he was asked to locate the graves of fallen soldiers so they could be removed to the main cemetery.

In addition to his government pension of thirty-four dollars a month, Mechlin returned to blacksmithing. In 1911, he moved into the United States Soldiers Home in Washington, D.C., where he died in 1926. He was buried there. His family remained in Mount Pleasant. His daughter Minnie went to live with the Hauser family on a local farm, where she earned her keep by doing chores.

The Story Within the Story

There is always as story within a story. As I was writing the first part of the historical society's insight into Henry Mechlin, my friend MaryBeth Hauser was in the process of cleaning up some papers. She found an envelope that was the mother lode of the Mechlin family. Among the treasures in the envelope were two letters, written by Minnie to the Hausers, remembering both her father and her time with them. Of her father, ninety-year-old Minnie said:

> *Where the Dough Boy is my father had a Blacksmith shop on the corner of I believe Main and Diamond. I don't know what is there now some time ago a long building that sold dishes...My Dad later bought a place in Laurelville from Van Horn and erected a Blacksmith shop there. Where the 3rd Ward School is...In my younger years Dad and Mom bought a Home from Jance Hawkeye right across from the School...Jance Hawkeye had a Daughter who married a Dr. Cowan from Greensburg. My brother sold the Dr my Dad's Carbean (Gun). I have been on the hunt for it. Robt Trombetta, Ft Pitt Museum called me 2 or 3 years ago said He had it.*

That's all Minnie told us in her letter. The Fort Pitt Museum did not have it. Another history mystery. Where is Henry Mechlin's gun? The state archives also had no trace of the gun. The Quartermaster's Museum in Virginia remembered Minnie. They had her come down on several occasions for various celebrations. No gun there either. Nor does the battlefield in Wyoming have the gun, but they knew of another mystery: Henry's Medal of Honor medal was also missing.

The Quartermaster's Museum acknowledged that Mechlin's original Medal of Honor also turned up missing in action. According to them, his daughter Minnie was too trusting and gave it to a military man who promised to get it appraised and then he disappeared. The family received a second one from the government, and it is now on display at the Battlefield museum in Montana. (Whoever has the medal can never try to sell it because Mechlin's name is on the back and the theft is a federal offense.) The Quartermaster's Museum have honored Mechlin by naming their water training site, still used to train the military, in his honor.

Among the Mechlin treasures were a number of items belonging to that famous Sioux chief, Sitting Bull. After Big Horn, the Sioux, like all the Indian nations, continued to fight against western expansion as long as they could. Eventually they had to give up. Mechlin was there as Sitting Bull brought his braves into Fort Buford. At some point, Mechlin acquired the great chief's bow and arrows, as well as his bear claw necklace. They are on display at the battlefield museum.

And the carbine? It probably went to Arizona with Dr. Cowan and is probably still there.[*]

Henry Mechlin is a Mount Pleasant hero. Not only because he did a brave thing at a famous battle, but also because when it was over, he returned home, pick up his hammer and became an ordinary citizen again, just like thousands of other American soldiers through the years.

---

* There is another local connection to the Henry Mechlin saga. There were few overland routes in the region, so the Yellowstone and Little Big Horn Rivers were used to transport supplies and perform other tasks. The steamboat that accompanied Custer's expedition was called the *Far West*. As with nearly 50 percent of all steamboats plying the western waters, the *Far West* was built along the Monongahela River, probably in California, Pennsylvania. The small boatbuilding centers of Brownsville, California, Belle Vernon and Monongahela had mastered the construction of the shallow hull. That opened the western waters. The *Far West*'s journey became legendary when it transported the wounded of the battle back to Fort Lincoln. On that trip, which broke all river records, the *Far West* covered the 920 miles back from the Little Big Horn to Fort Lincoln in fifty-four hours—a record-breaking time.

Notes

Chapter I

1. Archer Butler Hulbert, *Braddock Road and Three Relative Papers*, Historic Highways of America, Vol. 4 (Cleveland, OH: Arthur H. Clark Co. 1903), 53.
2. Winthrop Sargent, *The History of an Expedition Against Fort Du Quesne in 1755*, Historical Society of Pennsylvania (Philadelphia: J.B. Lippincott and Company, 1856), 346.
3. John Kennedy Lacock, "Braddock Road," *Pennsylvania Magazine of History and Biography* 37 (1914): 28.
4. George Fry Lee, *Westmoreland County History from a Mount Pleasant Township Perspective* (Greensburg, PA: Baltzer Meyer Historical Society, 1999), 5.
5. Paul A. Wallace, "'Blunder Camp': A Note on Braddock Road," Reprinted for the *Pennsylvania Historical and Museums Commission from the Pennsylvania Magazine of History and Biography* 87, no. 1 (January 1963): 24. Reprint from *PMHB* 28 (1914): 1–38. The survey mentioned in the quote is from: Survey D 46–100, Bureau of Land Records, Harrisburg, 1787 in pursuance of an order of survey dated April 3, 1769.
6. Norman Baker, *Braddock's Road: Mapping the British Expedition from Alexandria to the Monongahela* (Charleston, SC: The History Press, 1913).
7. Lacock, "Braddock Road," 27.
8. Sargent, *History of an Expedition*, 345.

9. *Connellsville Coke*, Pittsburgh: H.C. Frick Company, 1893.

10. *Mount Pleasant Journal* (Mount Pleasant, PA), "A Model of the Model," March 28, 1893.

11. *Connellsville Courier* (Connellsville, PA), "Report of the Operation and Output of the Coke Ovens of the Connellsville Region for the week ending Saturday, May 21, 1892," May 27, 1892, 2.

12. *Connellsville Courier* (Connellsville, PA), "Frick Exhibit: Two Complete Working Models to be Exhibited at the World's Fair," May 27, 1892, 2.

13. Joseph L. Morris, "What I Saw in the Coke Region," *Ohio Mining Journal* 23 (1894): 12–20: 14. https://kb.osu.edu/dspace/bitstream/handle/1811/32688/OH_MIN_JNL_v23_012.pdf?sequence=4.

14. "Letter from H.C. Frick to Thomas Lynch," October 4, 1893, *Helen Clay Frick Collection*, AIS.2002.06. Series XIII. H.C. Frick Coke Company, 1871–1921, Box 517, Vol. 5, Letterpress Copy Book 5, February 9, 1893–June 17, 1895, p. 118.

15. "Letter from H.C. Frick to Mr. C. A. Duniway, Cambridge, Mass.," November 11, 1893, *Helen Clay Frick Collection*, AIS.2002.06. Series XIII. H.C. Frick Coke Company, 1871–1921, Box 517, Vol. 5, Letterpress Copy Book 5, February 9, 1893–June 17, 1895, p. 127.

16. George Dallas Albert, "Coke," *History of the County of Westmoreland* (Philadelphia: L.H. Everts and Company, 1882), 403–414: 408.

CHAPTER II

17. George Harvey, *Henry Clay Frick: The Man* (New York: Charles Scribner's Sons, 1928), 55–57.

18. French Strother, "Frick, the Silent," *The World's Work*, Vol. 14, May 1907 to October 1907, in *A History of Our Time* (New York: Doubleday, Page & Company, 1907), 8849–58.

19. John Aubrey Enman, *The Relationship of Coal Mining and Coke Making to the Distribution of Population Agglomerations in the Connellsville (Pennsylvania) Beehive Coke Region* (PhD diss., University of Pittsburgh, 1963), 160.

20. Jill Cook, *The Town That Grew at the Crossroads* (Mount Pleasant, PA: Mount Pleasant Area Historic Preservation Committee, 1995), 26–27.

21. Secretary of Internal Affairs, *Annual Report of the Secretary of Internal Affairs of the Commonwealth of Pennsylvania,* Industrial Statistics, vol. 13 (Harrisburg, PA: E.K. Meyers), 1885, 150b.

22. *Coal Field Directory and Mining Catalog, Pocket Edition of the Directory Section for the Year 1915 Together with an Alphabetical List of Coal Companies* (Pittsburgh: Keystone Consolidated Publishing Company, 1915), 381.

23. *Weekly Courier* (Connellsville, PA), "Bids Submitted for the Abandoned Mines in the Morgan Valley," February 28, 1918, 2.

24. Secretary of Internal Affairs, "Reports of the Mine Inspectors of the Bituminous Coal Fields," Legislative Document No. 7, First, Second, and Fifth Districts in *Annual Report of the Secretary of the Internal Affairs of the Commonwealth of Pennsylvania,* Part III, Industrial Statistics, Vol. 11, 1882–83, 7a–153a, 132a.

25. *Keystone Courier* (Connellsville, PA), February 4, 1881.

26. Enman, *Relationship of Coal Mining,* 200.

27. *Coal Field Directory,* 1915, 381.

28. *Weekly Courier* (Connellsville, PA), "The Abandoned Mines in the Morgan Valley," February 28, 1918, 2.

29. Inspectors of Mines, *Reports of the Inspectors of Mines of the Anthracite and Bituminous Coal Regions of Pennsylvania, for the year 1888* (Harrisburg: Edwin K. Meyers, 1889), 349.

30. *Connellsville Courier* (Connellsville, PA), September 13, 1889, 2.

31. *Daily Courier* (Connellsville, PA), "Human Interest: Sidelights and Comments on Happenings Out of the Ordinary. Adelaide Home-Coming Stirs Old Memories," October 16, 1953, 12.

32. "Obituary: James Asa Childs," *Coal Age* 9 (January 1–June 30, 1916), 475.

33. *Evening Standard* (Uniontown, PA), "Another Quiet Day: A Big Slav Helps Sheriff McCormick Evict Yesterday," April 28, 1891, 1; *Morning Herald* (Uniontown, PA), "This Morning's Matchbox, Culver, Clover: Retrospect Items Dating to 1891," May 17, 1918, 4.

34. *Connellsville Courier* (Connellsville, PA), May 8, 1891, 1.

35. Ibid., September 6, 1889, 8.

36. *Morning Herald* (Uniontown, PA), "Frick Pensioners Receive $58,231.43," January 28, 1915, 1.

37. *Daily Courier* (Connellsville, PA), "Human Interest: Sidelights and Comments on Happenings Out of the Ordinary. Adelaide Home-Coming Stirs Old Memories," October 16, 1953, 12.

38. *Weekly Courier* (Connellsville, PA), "List of Coke Ovens in the Connellsville District," December 27, 1917, 2; *Connellsville Courier*, December 25, 1918, 2; Ibid., November 27. 1919,2; Ibid., November 11, 1920, 2; Ibid., October15, 1925, 2.

39. *Fourth Industrial Directory of the Commonwealth of Pennsylvania*, Pennsylvania Department of Internal Affairs (Harrisburg, PA: JLL Kuhn, 1922) 863.

40. *Weekly Courier* (Connellsville, PA), "New Coal Companies," November 8, 1917, 1.

41. Enman, *Relationship of Coal Mining*, 437.

42. *Morning Herald* (Uniontown, PA), "Sheriff's Sales," August 17, 1923, 11.

43. Ibid., May 1, 1923, 1, 3.

44. *Daily News Standard* (Uniontown, PA), July 10, 1929, 1.

45. *Daily Courier* (Connellsville, PA), July 17, 1929, 6.

46. *Connellsville Courier* (Connellsville, PA), February 18, 1926, 2; Ibid., December 30, 1926, 2; Ibid., November 27, 1931, 16.

47. Ibid., March 1, 1934, 5.

48. *Daily Courier* (Connellsville, PA), "Treasurer's Sale of Seated Lands for Taxes Delinquent for the Years 1940, 1941, 1942 and 1943," March 30, 1946, 6.

49. AMR Clearinghouse, "Redstone Creek Abatement Survey Scarlift Report," *AMRClearinghouse.org*, Intro 5. http://www.amrclearinghouse. org/Sub/SCARLIFTReports/RedstoneCreekAbatementSurvey/ RedstoneCreekAbatementSurvey.htm, 44.

CHAPTER IV

50. "John Brashear to Henry Clay Frick," June 2, 1903, University of Pittsburgh, Helen Clay Frick Foundation Archives.

51. "John Brashear to Henry Clay Frick," January 8, 1904, University of Pittsburgh, Helen Clay Frick Foundation Archives.

Bibliography

Albert, George Dallas. *History of the County of Westmoreland*. Philadelphia: L.H. Everts and Company, 1882.

Amphlet, William. *The Emigrant's Directory to the Western States or North America*. London: Longman, Hurst, Ress, Orme and Brown, 1819.

AMR Clearinghouse. "Redstone Creek Abatement Survey Scarlift Report." *AMRClearinghouse.org*. Intro 5. http://www.amrclearinghouse.org/Sub/SCARLIFTReports/RedstoneCreekAbatementSurvey/RedstoneCreekAbatementSurvey.htm.

Baker, Norman. *Braddock Road: Mapping the British Expedition from Alexandria to the Monongahela*. Charleston, SC: The History Press, 2013.

Charleroi Mail (Charleroi, PA). "Mrs. Hirvonen Tells Story of Harrowing Scenes in Latest Great Ocean Disaster." April 23, 1912.

Coal and Coke Campus. "West Leisenring, PA (Leisenring No. 2)." *Coal and Coke Campus*. http:// www.coalcampusa.com/westpa/connellsville/leisenring2/leisenring2.htm.

Coal Field Directory and Mining Catalog, Pocket Edition of the Directory Section for the Year 1915 Together with an Alphabetical List of Coal Companies. Pittsburgh: Keystone Consolidated Publishing Company, 1915.

Connellsville Courier (Connellsville, PA). "Frick Exhibit: Two Complete Working Models to be Exhibited at the World's Fair." May 27, 1892.

———. "Reports of the Operation and Output of the Coke Ovens of the Connellsville Region." N.d.

Cook, Jill. *The Town That Grew at the Crossroads*. Mount Pleasant, PA: Mount Pleasant Area Historic Preservation Committee, 1995.

Daily Courier (Connellsville, PA).

Daily News Standard (Uniontown, PA), July 10, 1929, 1.

Dwight, Margaret Van Horn. *A Journey to Ohio in 1810, as Recorded in the Journal of Margaret Van Horn Dwight*. Project Gutenburg. http://www.gutenberg.org/ebooks/36126.

Enman, John Aubrey. *The Relationship of Coal Mining and Coke Making to the Distribution of Population Agglomerations in the Connellsville (Pennsylvania) Beehive Coke Region*. PhD diss., University of Pittsburgh Library, 1963.

Evening Standard (Uniontown, PA). "Another Quiet Day: A Big Slav Helps Sheriff McCormick Evict Yesterday." April 28, 1891, 1.

Fourth Industrial Directory of the Commonwealth of Pennsylvania. Pennsylvania Department of Internal Affairs. Harrisburg, PA: JLL Kuhn, 1922.

Fry Lee, George. *Westmoreland County History from a Mount Pleasant Township Perspective*. Greensburg, PA: Baltzer Meyer Historical Society, 1999.

Galley, Henrietta, and J.O. Arnold, MD. *The History of the Galley Family with Local and Old-Time Sketches in the Yough Region*. Internet Archive. https://archive.org/details/historyofgalleyf00lcgall.

Harvey, George. *Henry Clay Frick: The Man*. New York: Charles Scribner's Sons, 1928.

Helen Clay Frick Foundation Archives. University of Pittsburgh.

Hulbert, Archer Butler. *Braddock Road and Three Relative Papers*. Historic Highways of America. Vol. 4. Cleveland, OH: Arthur H. Clark Company, 1903.

Inspectors of Mines. *Reports of the Inspectors of Mines of the Anthracite and Bituminous Coal Regions of Pennsylvania, for the year 1888*. Harrisburg, PA: Edwin K. Meyers, 1889.

Keystone Courier (Connellsville, PA).

Lacock, John Kennedy. "Braddock Road." *Pennsylvania Magazine of History and Biography* 37 (1914): 28.

Monessen Daily Independent (Monessen, PA).

Morning Herald (Uniontown, PA).

Morris, Joseph L. "What I Saw in the Coke Region." *Ohio Mining Journal* 23 (1894): 12–20: 14. https://kb.osu.edu/dspace/bitstream/handle/1811/32688/OH_MIN_JNL_v23_012.pdf?sequence=4.

Mount Pleasant Journal (Mount Pleaseant, PA).

Niemela, Juha, of the Institute of Migration. *Piispankatu* 3, 20500 Turku, Finland. www.utu.fi/eriull/instmigr.

Nummi, Gerald E., and Janet A. White. *I'm Going to see What Has Happened: The Personal Experience of 3rd Class Finnish* Titanic *Survivor, Mrs. Elin Hakkarainen.* N.p.: self-published, 1996.

"Obituary: James Asa Childs," *Coal Age* 9, (January 1–June 30, 1916), 475.

Sargent, Winthrop. *The History of an Expedition Against Fort Du Quesne in 1755.* Historical Society of Pennsylvania. Philadelphia: J.B. Lippincott and Company, 1856.

Searight, Thomas. *The Old Pike.* Uniontown, PA: self-published, 1894.

Secretary of Internal Affairs. *Annual Report of the Secretary of Internal Affairs of the Commonwealth of Pennsylvania.* Industrial Statistics. Vol. 13. Harrisburg, PA: E.K. Meyers, 1885.

Strother, French. "Frick, the Silent." *The World's Work,* Vol. 14, May 1907 to October 1907. In *A History of Our Time.* New York: Doubleday, Page & Company, 1907, 8849–58.

Wallace, Paul A. "'Blunder Camp': A Note on Braddock Road." Reprinted for the *Pennsylvania Historical and Museums Commission from the Pennsylvania Magazine of History and Biography* 87, no. 1 (January 1963).

Weekly Courier (Connellsville, PA).

Vivian, Cassandra. *Monessen: A Typical Steel Country Town.* Making of America Series. Charleston, SC: Arcadia Publishing, 2002.

———. "Monessen's Italians." *Il Primo Magazine* (Winter 2002).

———. *The National Road in Pennyslvania.* Images of America Series. Charleston, SC: Arcadia Publishing, 2003.

———. Our Town Remembered. *Mount Pleasant Journal,* 2010–12.

———. Titanic*: The Monessen Story.* Humanities in the Arts Grant of the Pennsylvania Council on the Arts and the Pennsylvania Humanities Council, 2000.

———. *A Walking and Driving Tour of Historic Brownsville.* Brownsville, PA: BARC, 1994.

Vivian, Cassandra, and Elizabeth Vivian and Vivian Pelini Sansone. *A Tuscan America Kitchen.* Gretna, PA: Pelican Press, 2011.

About the Author

Cassandra Vivian is a writer, photographer, lecturer, historian, educator and more. She has founded two historical societies and two museums, both still existing. Her collection of artifacts and photographs are housed at the Carnegie Museum of Natural History. She has appeared in two films on two continents. She has won numerous awards, including a meritorious award for lifetime achievement in publishing and the arts from her university.

Cassandra grew up on the fringes of the Laurel Highlands but lived her life on three continents and enjoyed every minute of it. Cassandra has written over twenty books on myriad subjects, but mostly on Western Pennsylvania, Egypt and Italian-Americans. She has consulted for PBS films and brought HABS/HAER of the National Parks Service to conduct an industrial archaeology survey of the Pittsburgh Steel Company facilities in Monessen. She gets things done.